DIVIDING THE GREAT

- from the not-so-great

By John Metcalfe

Acknowledgements:

A big thanks to John Kelly for putting up with me during our journey.

A lot of people helped me bring this book to fruition whether it was directly (like Dick Dodge and the plethora of kind people on the trail), or indirectly such as my family and friends whose faith in me was an inspiration when things got tough. For your selfless support I thank you.

I would like to acknowledge the vision and hard work of Adventure Cycling (www.adventurecycling.org) who mapped the Great Divide Mountain Bike Route and published the essential trail guide.

CANADA

North

Port of Roosville

Great Divide Route

Whitefish

Montana

Continental Divide

Helena

Butte

Idaho

Yellowstone

Jackson

Wyoming

South Pass City

Rawlins

Silverthorne

Utah

Salida

Colorado

Platoro

Cuba

Arizona

New Mexico

Pie Town

Silver City

Antelope Wells

MEXICO

PROLOGUE

'this magic has never diminished'

My love affair with cycling began when I was three years old. It was the first time that I cycled unassisted and experienced the magic of riding a bicycle. I was somehow able to slip my father's stabilising hold on my saddle and make my first few independent pedal strokes. As I grew older, being able to ride under my own steam literally broadened my horizons. It meant that I could explore new places, the length of my street, the next block, and go beyond the parameters that my mother had so austerely set. Cycling was to become a compelling force that fused together my ability to explore, to be self-sufficient and to meet new people. For me this magic has never diminished; even now whenever I mountain bike, commute to work, or just ride to the shops I still experience that addictive, childlike excitement.

As was the case with my inaugural two-wheeled experience, the blissful state of self-propulsion is generally accompanied by its antithesis: crashing. Yet despite my inability to stay upright, cycling has featured heavily in my life, and for some unknown reason I decided from an early age that I was going to be a professional cyclist. Such a decision was easy to make, I was young, pro-riders were old, so I had plenty of time before I had to do anything serious about my newly decided vocation. Until then I was content to just ride my bike for fun.

Of course the years have slipped under my wheels and I have done very little about realising my childhood dream. Even now, in my thirties, I find myself hanging on to scraps of information gleaned from the cycling press about riders in their forties who are doing well in the professional ranks. I use these little gems to bolster my flagging reverie and buy myself even more time before the bubble bursts. But the truth of the matter is, I am no athlete. I lack the physiology and resoluteness to be even a journeyman cyclist let alone a pro. That said I have been blessed with one exceptional quality that has proved invaluable during my sketchy cycling career, a phenomenally poor long-term memory. A case in point was my thirtieth birthday. With more than a hint of a premature – or an immature – midlife crisis, and a need to strengthen my dream, I celebrated my anniversary by entering the solo category of a 24 hour mountain bike race. As the sun rose midway through the race, and I became a year older, my body was undergoing a trauma equalled only in magnitude to that which it endured on the same day three

5

decades earlier. I vowed to myself at that moment that I would never ride a bike again. Yet once the race was over and the sense of doom had receded, my substandard short-term memory was unable to render the earlier horrors and I found myself planning strategies for the following year. It is this Etch-a-Sketch ability to delete pain from my memory that enables me to keep getting on my bike.

I am also incredibly good at procrastinating. On average it takes about six years for an idea to become a reality, more if the task is difficult, with the option that it might be indefinite should it require a lot of effort. As a result my cycling to-do list is as long as my arm and is growing exponentially as my idling brain comes up with new two-wheeled feats that are clearly beyond my physiology or verve. The ideal antidote to such an apathetic lack of success is to compare yourself to others of a similar, or preferably, worse disposition. John Kelly, or JK as he likes to be known, was an ideal candidate for my comparative cycling partner. All of his claims collapsed under the slightest scrutiny; he had achieved very little, exaggerated what he had done and had plenty to say about what he was going to do. Of course the relationship is symbiotic, he provides the perfect alibi for me and I for him.

For any serious and also wannabe endurance mountain biker, the Great Divide Mountain Bike Route is the jewel in the crown. It stretches from Canada to Mexico and is considered America's premier long-distance mountain bike trail by the Adventure Cycling Association. The route starts at the Port of Roosville on the Montana-British Columbia border and follows the Continental Divide – as closely as possible – down to Antelope Wells at the New Mexico-Mexico border. The Continental Divide is an imaginary line that separates the flow of water on the continent. On the west side of the line water runs into the Pacific Ocean, whereas on the east it flows into the Atlantic. Put another way, the Great Divide follows the Rockies which means plenty of ups, downs and everything in between.

Being wannabes, it stands to reason that the Great Divide was our to-do lists. My main concern was that it stood a serious chance of not getting completed, especially when we were shelving easier, domestic long-distance rides for nebulous reasons. Drastic action was therefore needed. On the odd occasion that I have achieved my cycling objectives, I have found two motivation tools useful. The first is financial the second is verbal.

I phoned JK.

'So we're still on for the Great Divide?' I inquired.

'You bet…definitely this year,' came his blasé reply.

6

'Good, so you won't mind giving me your credit card details.'

'WHAT?' (I suspected the trepidation in JK's voice was because somewhere in his rational mind he feared the Great Divide plan was being galvanised).

'I've been on the Internet and found some decent priced flights...' I offered, and noticing an apologetic tone to my voice, I sternly added '...so there's no reason why we shouldn't book them.'

Cornered, JK had no choice, to back out now would expose him for the charlatan that he really is. So he did the honourable thing and proffered his credit card details. It was an adroit move because in saving his face he had also called my bluff. Faced with no other options I completed our details on the electronic form and clicked submit. That was it; the tickets were on their way. We had to do it.

The second stage of goal fulfilment is to get on your soapbox and tell everyone what you're planning to do. And to ensure a vicious tongue-lashing if you don't complete your mission, it's often necessary to decry everyone else for not attempting it themselves. I took to this task enthusiastically, and was so convincing I even started to believe the audacious claims I was making. Of course I was writing a substantial verbal cheque that I was unsure my body could cash; perfect preparation for the trip.

Running in tandem with my childhood dream of becoming a professional cyclist I've also got a rather optimistic theory about my athletic potential. It is not a product of intense research, rather it has developed in my subconscious mind over the years and has resided there for so long that I have come to believe that it is true. At best it is half-baked, but it is a theory nonetheless. It goes something like this: I am half as good as any World Class athlete. For example: I can run a marathon or the 100m sprint inside double the respective world record times. Extrapolating this means that I should also be able to complete the Great Divide in twice the record time. The current holder of this record is John Stamstad – a legendary ultraendurance mountain biker – who rode the 2500 miles unassisted in eighteen days and five hours. To put his achievement in perspective, the distance he rode was further than the Tour de France and he did it in less time. Furthermore he carried all of his equipment and didn't have the assistance of team mechanics, soigneurs and the usual Tour de France accoutrements. Using this as a yardstick I calculated that we should be able to get from Canada to Mexico in about thirty seven days, or six weeks at the outside. Of course my theory does not hold up well under scrutiny, because there is no way I could get round eighteen holes of golf in double what Tiger Woods can, nor would it be feasible for me to go half the distance with Lennox Lewis. But I choose to ignore these bothersome anomalies.

Now the flights were booked, my motivation seemed to be roused. I circled our departure date on my year planner above my desk and was stirred into action by how little time there was. It was a little over four months, or four thin columns on my planner which meant we had to move like we had a purpose. We had sixteen weeks to prepare for the trip and get ourselves in shape. Attempting the Great Divide in thirty seven days meant we would have to cover anywhere between sixty and one hundred miles each day. I had ridden these kinds of distances before, but never on consecutive days, so it was time to test our mettle.

Our acid test was to be the Wessex Way, the longest off-road, coast to coast mountain bike ride in Britain. The route links some of the oldest ridge roads and cart tracks in Europe, taking the traveller 250 miles across the ancient kingdom of its namesake. It begins in Weston in the southwest and extends as far as Eastbourne in the southeast. If we could complete it in three days we would be on target, if not then we would be scuppered (with hindsight it probably would have been wise to attempt this prior to handing over our hard-earned cash to the airline, but that would have been logical).

On a cold March morning, whilst the seaside town of Weston was still asleep, we set off from the Grand Pier. After only a few turns of the cranks we were pulling off the tarmac and onto the bridleway leading up Worlebury Hill. In doing so we left the Bristol Channel behind, and with a bit of luck the next expanse of water we'd encounter would be the English Channel at the opposite end of our journey. Despite the laden bikes, we covered our planned eighty miles on the first day and were in relatively good spirits. That is until the first night's camp, it was a cold one, well at least for me it was. JK was cocooned in his brand new three-season down sleeping bag whilst mine was a few seasons short of the mark. In my quest for lightness I had sacrificed a bit of comfort and with hindsight I would have gladly traded half-a-kilo for a couple of degrees of warmth. In the morning I bartered with JK for the use of his duvet jacket for the following night. It cost me a couple of Mars bars but it seemed a small price to pay. *Mental note #1: pack a warmer sleeping bag next time.*

Riding across Golden Ball Hill at sunrise was an inspirational experience and I readily forgot the discomfort of the previous night's camp. With my morale boosted we set about our task of getting another eighty miles on the odometer. We were adapting well to life on the trail, especially the alfresco dining which generally consisted of snacks from petrol stations. Fortunately I had been given the carte blanche by my waistline to eat all of the chocolate I wanted because my legs were burning it off. Again we completed our planned eighty miles with few impediments, but the camp proved irksome - JK's sleeping bag was conspicuous by its absence. It was originally riding piggyback atop my rack pack. Now there was just my rack pack, the sleeping bag must have abandoned ship somewhere along the trail. Instantly I interpreted the situation, no duvet jacket for me tonight. *Mental note #2: securely lash down mental note #1.*

The following morning my motivation for finishing the Wessex Way in three days had changed somewhat. Originally it was to prove that we were up for the Great Divide, now it was to avoid another cold night without a sleeping bag. Judging by the pace that JK had set off he was also inspired by the prospect of not having to camp again. We frenetically covered the remaining ninety miles and arrived in Eastbourne as it was getting dark. Yet apart from my sleeping bag faux pas and our need to cram as much food into our stomachs as possible, we were in good shape and I was secretly impressed by our performance. Then, without so much as a word, JK sprinted off into the night in search of food. I just managed to stick on his wheel all of the way to a late night greasy spoon where we systematically worked our way through the menu. As I got up after our protracted refectory break I felt a twinge in my knee, no doubt brought about by the reckless sprinting that was not becoming of a man of my years. Little did I know it then, but it was the beginning of an injury that was going to give me some concern.

Indeed my knee injury kicked in for earnest the next morning to such an extent that it meant that I would have to put my training on hold for a few weeks. Actually that is not strictly true. I had read somewhere that polar explorers fattened up before their expeditions in order to counteract the vast amounts of energy they would expend. I took this as read and during my physical lay-off I set about my dietary training with all the vigour of someone half my age.

I learned two major things during my Wessex Way assignment. Firstly equipment choice was paramount, and secondly my arse hurt after consecutive days on the trail. The first issue was pretty straightforward to sort out, most of the kit I already owned was suitable, and I didn't mind asking for help for the one or two upgrades I needed. But whom do you ask about the arse thing? I spent half an hour one Saturday morning in the embrocation section of my local road cycling shop. Like a teenager in a chemist I felt distinctly uneasy and was trying to work out what to say to the assistant when a booming voice over my right shoulder nearly startled me into knocking down a precarious pyramid of liniments. 'Don't bother with them, waste o'money.'

I spun round to see a fit, weather-beaten veteran in full cycling regalia, who looked like he'd been cycling for the last fifty years without ever stopping.

'Oh, right, yeah, I mean erm…' I nervously stammered.

'Never used t'stuff. Y'should take a leaf out the experts' book,' he said trying to make eye contact with me.

'Who are the experts?' I asked, looking up sheepishly.

'The nippers,' he replied, as if I should automatically know what he was on about, 'they are happy to sit in their own shit and piss all day. Get yourself some nappy cream from the chemist and fettle it around y'bits,' he bellowed whilst gesticulating the process.

His ample decibels and hand actions drew the attention of a few customers and a member of staff who looked at us in a scornful manner like only a librarian can when someone is disturbing the peace.

'Right. I will. Thanks,' I murmured and made my exit under the contemptuous glower of the shop assistant.

Fortunately, acquiring the cycling equipment was a far easier experience, socially speaking, than the nappy cream debacle, but was somewhat more destructive financially. My initial assessment of my existing kit being up to the task was naive in the extreme. To be honest it probably would have sufficed, but once I had entered the mesmerising world of outdoors equipment I was hooked. I had no idea that this marvellous parallel universe existed.

For some reason I had always assumed that technological advances in equipment, whatever the discipline, were driven by the space exploration industry, and that the stuff that us mere mortals use in our day-to-day lives such as Teflon were scraps left over from NASA's table. But it appears that this is not the case. Instead it turns out that it has been the outdoors equipment industry that has been silently pushing the technological envelope all these years. The proof is the vast array of new materials and gizmos bearing esoteric names: *3-ply Gortex, GPS, carbonfibre-Kevlar laminate, Primaloft,* and my personal favourite: *checktheamountandenteryourPIN.*

I am what the commission based outdoors salesman has been waiting for his entire career. When I walked into my local outdoors equipment shop I was about to make someone reach his monthly sales target in one fell swoop with minimum effort.

'Excuse me, can you tell me why this jacket is twice as expensive as this one?' I asked holding up what appeared to be two identical jackets. I might as well have said 'Hi, my name is Rich Pickings.'

According to his name badge I was dealing with Peter and it appeared that our Peter was no ordinary salesman; I was in the presence of an executive sales assistance. He looked at me like I had asked him what century we were in.

'The one in your right hand is more waterproof than the one in your left,' came his succinct reply.

I thought for a minute. Surely something is either waterproof or it isn't? It is not the sort of thing that can be placed on a continuum. I said as much, and regrettably with too much aloofness. I was shot down in flames with a verbatim retort of the manufacturer's catalogue blurb. It all sounded very impressive.

'I'm sorry, which one did you say was the best?' I asked Peter when he had finished his rendition.

'The one in your right hand.'

'Thanks I'll take it.'

As a result of a protracted Internet-based spending spree I received a deluge of parcels of varying sizes which I opened with all the zeal of a child on Christmas morning. I also found myself in a financial stranglehold. The initial £535 for the flight was in a way a bit like a non-returnable deposit, and it helped me galvanise my actions towards the trip. However, as I purchased more and more items it became more and more like a money extraction scam. One morning whilst reading the papers I was startled by the parallels of an article about a bunch of fraudsters who conned unsuspecting investors to part with their money. The idea behind the scam was to ask for a moderate amount of cash and promise a decent return in a year's time. The following year the fraudsters would inform the investors of the large sum that was owed to them, however to relinquish this sum the investors would have to cough up a 10% liberating fee. The process was repeated several times (substituting liberating fee with administration charges and so on) until, even though the investors suspected foul play, they had put so much money into the scam they couldn't afford to pull out and call it a day. Some lost their homes in the process. My scam however was a little less thought-out as it involved me talking myself out of large sums of money and handing it over to other businesses.

The most difficult aspect was deciding what to take. There seems to be two schools of thought when it comes to packing for the Great Divide: to take a trailer, or not take a trailer. Having used a trailer once before I was dead set against the idea. The situation had been very similar to our proposed ride; a hapless friend and myself had embarked on a doomed round-the-world trip on, wait for it, a tandem (I know it sounds like folly now, but at the time it seemed like the most appropriate mode of transport). The tandem with the trailer attached handled like an oil tanker and after negotiating each turn the whole contraption would wobble and resonate for an age afterwards. This caused a noticeable shearing effect and I hold it chiefly responsible for snapping the tandem in half about a hundred kilometres outside of Istanbul. Fortunately it happened near a petrol station and not having a penny between us we were forced to think on our feet. With careful preparation and using various propping aides, we managed to lean the tandem against a wall so that it looked like a complete bike. We then proceeded to trade the steed for a bottle of Coke, a few bags of crisps and a packet of chocolate digestives with an unsuspecting petrol station attendant. He was blissfully unaware of the dud that he had acquired and seemed extremely pleased with the transaction. Indeed he overtly wore the self-satisfying body language of a master dealer who had duped an unwitting customer. 'Ha, there's one born every minute,' I thought to myself trying to conceal a smirk.

Before our cover was blown we managed to flag down a lift to the city. We quickly threw our belongings into the back of the car and hurriedly instructed the driver to pull away. Through the rear window I watched the tandem and its new owner disappear into the distance and as soon as I was sure we were a safe distance away from any reprisals a warm wave of one-upmanship washed over me. I unwrapped our newly acquired biscuits and bit into a horribly stale, dud digestive. There's one born every minute.

Another reason I dislike trailers is because they are heavy, cumbersome, require extra spares and they encourage you to pack more stuff – purely because you can. Moreover, in his record setting attempt, John Stamstad went sans trailer, so it was clearly the way to go.

To carry my gear I opted for a bar bag, a frame bag and an Ortllieb waterproof sausage bag that fitted atop my rear rack. This minimal carrying space meant that everything I packed was chosen on merit. There were no luxuries, just essentials. My pride and joy was an Airborne titanium frame called Corsair; it was to be the heart of my bike to which everything, including my dream, was to be fastened.

CHAPTER ONE. GETTING STARTED

'destinations are overrated'

'You'll never do it. It's too many miles.'

I don't know why his statement shocked me, what else should I have expected from a customs official with a fifty inch waist? Nonetheless it was a fantastic welcome to the Land Of Opportunity.

'Where are you staying?' he asked without looking up.

'I'll be camping on the trailside,' I explained.

He eyeballed me po-faced.

'I need an address, where are you staying?'

'Well, I haven't got an address, I'm going to be camping...'

'Step back from the line Sir and complete the address box on the form.'

'But, I don't have an address...' I began.

'STEP BACK FROM THE LINE,' he repeated sternly. I was acutely aware that I had been demoted from Sir. Our slight altercation was drawing the attention of the queuing passengers, some of whom were enjoying the spectacle, others were annoyed at being held up. I began to feel a little self-conscious as if, for example, I had asked him for some nappy cream. From the other side of the checkpoint, JK, who had got through without a problem, was smirking and tapping his watch as if he was in a hurry. I was pleased to see he was enjoying the scene. Without wanting to antagonise the situation any further I rejoined the queue and wrote Days Inn as my address. Luckily, there were four customs desks open and with a bit of timely stalling I managed to avoid the troublesome bureaucrat and got a kind hearted motherly type instead. Upon hearing of my proposed adventure, she proceeded to tell me at length about her nephew's ventures on his bicycle. I nodded enthusiastically in all of the right places and she stamped my passport without question. I was in at last.

My recalcitrant knee injury had flared up as a result of the cramped conditions on the plane. So while we were waiting for our baggage I performed some stretches to loosen off the joint. This also provided a mild form of entertainment for the other passengers. It was then that I noticed a selection of my tool kit going round on the carousel accompanied by my Time Atac clipless pedals, which looked suspiciously like hand grenades. This was a little disconcerting as I had securely taped them to Corsair which I knew I had put inside a sturdy cardboard box. I quickly collected the offending items and shrugged my shoulders at JK.

'A bit worrying,' I muttered, 'I hope my bike's in one piece.'

'At least you've got something, I can't believe how long it is taking,' JK retorted in an uncharacteristically curt tone.

We stood in line and joined everyone else as they intently watched the rubber flap at the mouth of the carousel for any sign of movement. It had been a while since the last piece of luggage – my tool kit – had materialised. Then all of a sudden, accompanied by 'ooohs' and 'arhhhs' from the line up, the dam burst and our bike boxes, which must have been responsible for the hold up, burst out onto the carousel spewing luggage out behind them. Without thought for logic or organisation everyone dashed forward to retrieve their belongings. It reminded me of an experience I once had in India; I had just completed a gruelling fourteen hour journey spent cheek to jowl on an overcrowded train. When the train pulled into a station the majority of passengers were desperate to alight onto the platform. Of course everyone on the thronging platform desperately wanted to board the train. The obvious solution was for the passengers to get off before the others embarked, however logic did not prevail, we spent an inordinate amount of time in stalemate. A similar mêlée occurred at the carousel, but we somehow managed to salvage our unwieldy boxes and regroup in a quiet section of the reclaim-baggage lobby. It was a sorry sight, my bike box had an alarming curvature along its length (I just hoped there was a straight section through which my bike had managed to survive), and JK's box looked liked it had been kicked here all the way from the UK.

'I can't believe it has only been on and off *one* plane,' he scowled.

And in a fit of infuriation he kicked it.

This was only part one of our four leg journey to the trailhead. We were in Atlanta International airport and were scheduled to fly to Seattle tomorrow. The bikes, whose job it was in a few days to liberate us from the shackles of modern life, were proving to be albatrosses around our necks. It proved impossible to move around with two cardboard boxes each one the size of a mattress. A simple task like negotiating escalators, doors and even people, quickly degenerated into a Laurel and Hardy type sketch, only I didn't find it too funny. Shortly after being told at the information desk that there was no baggage storage facility in light of the September 11th tragedy, we stumbled across the baggage storage counter which was fully operational and open for business. Delighted at the prospect of being freed from our unwieldy baggage, we dragged the shredded bike boxes to the counter where we were faced with a phenomenally ignorant individual.

'Can we leave these here for the night?' JK asked the attendant.

Without taking his eyes off a battered black and white TV the attendant slapped a form down on the counter.

'I take it you want me to fill this out,' JK rhetorically muttered.

'Forty dollars,' came the reply.

'Christ, do they get an en suite for that?' I chipped in.

The attendant didn't acknowledge my sarcasm, instead he chose to fix his attention firmly on the cheesy game show that was losing a battle with interference for screen space. It didn't bode well. I had initially thought that we would be able to get a motel room for $40, but if that was the going rate for a couple of bikes then my budget of $500 cash for the whole trip suddenly seemed woefully inadequate. I handed over the cash and my request for a receipt was met with a stony silence. As we walked away the attendant slapped his hand on the counter. I turned to see him gesture that he wanted us to carry the bikes through to the back. Forty dollars and he expected us to lug the stuff around? He must be joking, surely? The attendant trained his eyes back on the TV. He obviously wasn't.

It had been a long, tiring day and it was getting late when we finally caught a cab to the nearest motel. I lay back on my bed and reflected on the situation, it was good to be in the States and get the ball rolling, I was in good spirits and despite my truculent knee, I didn't feel too bad considering I hadn't slept well in two days. Having said that, I don't normally fall asleep fully clothed.

I awoke the next morning to JK scurrying around the motel room.

'What's the rush mate?' I groggily inquired.

'Didn't you see the sign?'

I glanced around the room looking for a "You must vacate the room by…" sign, but there wasn't one.

'What sign?'

'The one in reception about the complimentary breakfast,' he replied as he made his way out of the door.

About an hour later I joined JK in the reception for what was to become a habitual "continental" breakfast. They generally consisted of four doughnuts and as many coffee refills as we could stomach.

'It's bloody hot out there,' I said between bites of what appeared to be triple-fried, sugar-coated stodge. 'I think I'll get my hair shaved off before we catch the flight, it'll be murder on the bike otherwise.'

15

'Do you want my two pennies worth?' JK offered without breaking stride as he devoured another doughnut.

'Fire away.'

'I'd keep it long,' he advised, glancing around for a napkin to mop up the jam he'd spilt down the front of his T-shirt. Opting to suck the jam off he added, 'it's dreading up nice. Fancy another coffee refill?'

I followed JK's advice on both counts, I postponed my coiffing and I joined him on a couple of coffee refills. I eventually became nauseated by the effects of free coffee overindulgence and decided to give up full strength coffee. My reasoning was caffeine has a diuretic effect and exacerbates dehydration, which was something we would need to avoid in potential draught areas of the ride. Of course I wasn't going to give up coffee altogether – thank God for decaf.

Checking the bikes back in at the airport was a lot less hassle than I had anticipated; no cranky attendants, no one with a tape measure complaining that it was one inch too long demanding that I'd have to pay an excess $1000 fee. No, it was as easy as a check-in is supposed to be. However, I was a little perturbed when the guy operating the X-ray machine stopped the conveyer belt while Corsair was being scanned and called his mate over. They found the X-ray image of Corsair highly amusing. They looked at their monitor then looked at me and laughed. I couldn't be arsed asking them what was funny, I needed a beer. Our swift check-in meant we had a couple of hours to kill and what better place than at Atlanta airport's own Houlihan's bar? Well, any bar that sells cheap beer would be a start. It had the oxymoron title of being a sports bar and was filled with fat, clearly unfit, unhealthy people watching sports, drinking beer and eating fat. Perfect. We squeezed in, pulled up a couple of barstools, drank beer and chewed the fat as well as ate it. A newscaster on the TV above the bartender's head interrupted our conversation when he informed us that our airline had the worst maintenance record in the US.

JK was philosophical. 'At least they know about it now.'

I tried to be pragmatic. 'If we're going to crash I'd sooner it was on our next flight rather than the one back home. At least that way we won't have to ride two and a half thousand miles.'

Of course nothing happened, indeed it was uneventful, some (read JK) might say it was boring. The only surprise I had during the whole flight was that my mini-cheesecake tasted like cheesecake. The uneventful flight can in part be attributed to JK's topic of conversation following our in-flight meal. As with most airline food ours was accompanied by a moist towelette. Indeed we had the deluxe version, it was 'an extra-large towelette' according to the description on the packet. Well JK really sunk his teeth in to this one. He reasoned that a towelette is a small towel, therefore a large towelette was in fact a towel, and that an extra large towelette was a large towel. Therefore our large towelettes were really towels. There was no way I could get him off the subject, so I resorted to rereading my copy of the National Geographic whilst letting his theory go in one ear and out of the other.

My first impression of Seattle airport was that it was better than Atlanta. In fact it was $30 and a thank you better. It only cost us $10 to store the bikes and the attendant was pleasantry personified. With the bikes stowed away, we had the rest of the evening and the best part of the next day to relax before we were due to board the night train to Whitefish, Montana. Enthused by the free breakfasts, JK wanted to check out *all* of the motels to establish which one offered the best food. I wisely took a couple ibuprofens to ease my knee pain before we started the long search for our beds for the night. We settled on Econo Lodge by virtue of their doughnuts and decaf, but I didn't really get a chance to check out the room, because once again as soon as I lay down on my bed I fell asleep.

The following morning, with distended bellies, we left the breakfast table and waddled off in search of a cab. Somewhere in the back of my mind I wondered if this was how John Stamstad had prepared for his record attempt. I figured not, but I had read somewhere that his fuel of choice is fried Spam, so you never know. We got a taxi-van back to the airport to collect the bikes – which were now only protected by a threadbare cardboard exoskeleton – and got dropped off at the Amtrak train station. We dragged our decaying baggage into the loading bay.

'Jeez, you guys travelled far?' the check-in attendant asked eyeing up the beaten boxes.

'Would you believe they've only been on two planes?' JK asked.

'Sounds about right, those airport handlers,' the attendant said in a tone he only used for describing serfs, then added, 'you're going to have to put them in new boxes before they go on the train. There's a couple of boxes over there you can use.'

'Cheers.' I replied, and set about repacking our gear.

JK kicked his bike once more and furiously ripped the remaining cardboard away. 'Shit! My pedals have gone!' he shouted.

'Is everything alright guys?' asked the attendant as he tentatively peered over his counter.

17

'Yeah, everything is fucking great,' replied JK as he booted his cycling helmet halfway down the platform, 'they've only gone and lost my pedals.'

'Are you sure they're not in the box?' the attendant asked.

JK glared at him with violence in his eyes.

'We're not sure,' I interjected, 'we'll have a proper look.'

'There not in there,' JK hissed through clenched teeth.

'I know mate, but at least we found out now and not at the trailhead,' I reasoned, 'let's pack them up, have a decaf and get some new pedals from REI.'

We packed up the bikes, this time using a full roll of duct tape on each one and took them to the check-in desk.

'That's ten dollars please,' said the check-in guy.

JK handed over the cash and we sent the bikes on their way. As we walked off I asked JK what the $10 was for.

'Fuck knows, but I do know I need a coffee.'

We sat outside a Starbucks enjoying the mid-morning sun and the therapeutic effects of hazelnut decaf. The extra large blueberry muffins also helped. As we sat there, I watched the cycle couriers skilfully ride between the traffic and was impressed by their gracefully intense pace. A sticker on one of the bikes caught my eye, it read 'destinations are overrated'. The Buddhist connotations were lost on me, but I secretly hoped Antelope Wells, our destination, wasn't going to be a letdown.

'Jesus, what's that smell?' asked JK.

About one block over JK's right shoulder a gentleman of the road was inspecting the inside of a trash can for salvage. We were sitting downwind of him and bore the brunt of his unwashed odour. We didn't know it then, but that particular smell was going to feature heavily over the forthcoming weeks. Feeling nauseous, we quickly drained our coffees and headed for REI (Recreational Equipment Inc.) to look for some new pedals. REI's cycle department was an Aladdin's cave chockfull of mountain bike goodies. I exercised an unusual degree of self-discipline and somehow managed to keep my plastic firmly in my wallet. To be honest I couldn't purchase anything because I didn't have any carrying space left on my bike (another good reason for not taking a trailer). That said, I did inquire about the viability of purchasing a Litespeed frame and mailing it home. Unfortunately, or fortunately, it proved to be cost prohibitive. JK on the other hand was lured by the beauty and elegance of a pair of carbon Time Atac pedals and he also procured a pair of Cannondale cycling shoes because 'they go nicely with the pedals.'

Back outside the sun was getting into its stride, making it uncomfortably hot to just walk around. Yet despite the intense heat, I heeded JK's advice and avoided having a haircut. Instead we killed time in the fine coffee bars and delis of Seattle. Unfortunately my injured knee marred the ambience and I was becoming somewhat hacked off with it. Despite consuming ibuprofens like they were Smarties the pain still managed to breach the analgesic buffer, suggesting that the injury was getting worse. This was a little perturbing as I hadn't even started cycling. The only saving grace was that it only hurt when I was stationary and seemed to subside when I was moving. Obviously the last thing I needed was a prolonged bout of inactivity and of course, that was exactly what was next on the schedule. To ease the thought of the overnight, coach-class journey I consumed liberal amounts of medicinal Budweiser and to show what a loyal friend he is JK, despite not having an injury, did likewise. What a trooper he is.

The Amtrak train was an American classic. It was one of those really long ones that you see in the movies where the protagonist crosses the rail track just in front of the engine and the chasing cops have to wait an age for it to pass. The interior proved far better than I had imagined. My fears of cramped conditions and knee pain were allayed by the relative comfort (compared to the confined airplane flights); there was plenty of legroom, the seats fully reclined, and there was a dining coach that offered real meals rather than the ubiquitous American junk food. The only downside was that the train never got out of second gear, but that would have been out of character; it was slow, steady and comfortable - the ideal antidote to our previous frenetic schedule. Aware that dehydrated food was going to play a huge part in our daily diets over the coming weeks, we reserved a table for supper. Over the previous days I had developed an increasing desire for seafood and was pleased to find I would be able to satiate it with a nice baked trout. Reasoning that it was going to be our last decent meal I felt fully justified in ordering a double helping of cherry pie and ice cream. Of course it wasn't our last meal at all, there was breakfast the following morning, but that had somehow slipped my mind.

The gentle swaying of the train, the soporific effect of the meal and the compounded fatigue of several days travel, meant that I had a contented, dreamless sleep. I awoke the next morning feeling refreshed in my body, but the abstinence from caffeine was beginning to show. I was suffering from coffee drinkers' cold turkey and had an awful headache. However, I wasn't going to let it ruin my full English breakfast. I was pushing out the boat this morning because this was *definitely* the last decent meal I was going to have in a long time. Shortly after breakfast, Train 8 pulled into Whitefish, Montana station and we alighted onto the platform, which was bathed in glorious sunshine. We leaned on our bike boxes and watched the train slowly pull out of the station.

'Well this is it,' JK said then added, 'I'll go and ring for a taxi.'

Whilst JK made the call I dragged the boxes round to the front of the station, leant against the railings and waited for our lift.

'Of course I'm just going through the motions on this trip,' JK said wistfully as he joined me leaning on the railings.

'What?'

'Yeah, I've already done it, the whole thing,' he added.

'What are you on about?' He now had my full attention.

'I dreamt it the other day. I did the whole lot and got to Antelope Wells. I even know the colour of the cab that's coming. It's a black pickup,' he said gazing far into the distance.

'Was I there? Was I at Antelope Wells?' I inquired, wanting to know my fate.

'I can't say for sure. I was definitely there, but I don't know about you'. He faced me and added wisely, 'but I bet you the cab is a black pickup.'

CHAPTER TWO. FROM WHITEFISH TO WHITEFISH

'it was going to get worse. A lot worse'

'Either of you two John Kelly?' a middle aged man asked, leaning out of the driver's window of a large white panel van.

'That's me,' JK acknowledged.

'I'm Charlie, I'm your lift. I spoke to you on the phone.'

I gave JK a 'so much for the black pickup' expression.

He shrugged and countered it with a 'oh well there's no guarantees' look.

When we opened the rear doors of the van it became apparent that it was an inverse tardis; the loss of space inside was due to several rows of seats and an array of odds and ends. I'm not sure what Charlie was thinking about when he selected this van for the job, but he didn't seem at all fazed. Once again the boxes were traumatised as they were forced into spaces that were clearly too small. Despite Charlie's endless packing permutations, the boxes still hung over the edge of the van by a couple of inches preventing the doors from fully shutting. This little fact didn't perturb Charlie, who now opted for brute force and ignorance. I had to turn away when he repeatedly slammed the doors against the boxes with increasing vigour until the boxes yielded and the doors closed.

'No problem,' he said triumphantly rubbing his hands.

Eventually we set off and drove north through the pastoral farmlands of Tobacco Valley and got to Port of Roosville in just under two hours. The planning and preparation had seemingly taken ages and it was now good to be on the final leg of our journey to the trailhead. On route Charlie informed us that he had already given lifts to several riders and that we would probably be the last end-to-end bikers for the year. The Great Divide is a seasonal route and a successful journey is highly dependant upon the weather. According to the trail notes, at 1700 miles into the ride is the high altitude Indiana Pass through which there is a brief window when it is free of snow. Furthermore for a swift journey it is imperative to miss the rainy season in New Mexico. Due to our work commitments we didn't have the luxury of being able to pick our start date and as such had set off relatively late. Our belated start wasn't too perturbing because we were aiming to make up some time by travelling light and significantly reduce the guidebook recommended schedule of sixty two days.

Charlie pulled up in the parking lot outside a diner-cum-bar situated a few yards from the border checkpoint. As I climbed out of the van, the full juxtaposition of heat hit me. Three days ago I was in Manchester at sixty five degrees, here it was in the nineties and it was only half past ten in the morning. Noticing I was taken aback, Charlie informed me that the newspapers were predicting record temperatures over the next couple of days. I wasn't too sure why he was telling me this, it's not like I wanted to hear it.

'I was kind of hoping it was only going to get hot as we headed south,' I commented.

'Oh yeah, it'll get hotter there for sure. The whole country is cooking this year,' he said, with an air of national pride, or sadism, I couldn't tell.

He heaved our bikes out of the van and deposited them on the ground with all of the panache of an airport baggage handler. He climbed back into his air conditioned van, sipped coffee from a thermal mug and watched us rebuild our bikes. The heat was oppressive and I needed to sit down and take a breather. Of course I didn't because Charlie was watching. Instead I went about the task as enthusiastically as I could but I'm sure I didn't fool him. He must have realised that I shouldn't be sweating as much as I was by just strapping a few items onto a bike.

After what seemed like an age he finally wound down his window,

'Well I gotta get going, I've got another fare. Good luck gentlemen, all the best.'

We shook hands through the open window, and in a cloud of dust he headed south down Highway 93. I slumped back onto a nearby dumpster and exhaled loudly.

'Hell's teeth this is hot,' JK muttered shaking his head wistfully, 'fancy a Coke?'

I didn't need asking twice. We headed into the bar and ordered a couple of large Cokes with ice.

Seeing our knackered demeanour a barfly asked, 'you guys come far?'

Great, why did he have to ask this at the beginning of the journey? I went from mountain bike hero to fraud in a nanosecond; here I was having a break, sipping Coke and enjoying the air conditioning and I hadn't even finished building my bike.

'No but we're heading far.' I offered.

In a manner that suggested he only wanted to trade real, not perchance, travel tales he returned his attention to his Budweiser.

'Where are you stopping tonight?' the bartender asked JK, perhaps thinking we might want lodgings already.

'Tuchuck campground, about forty miles off,' JK replied.

'Better get a move on then,' said Barfly.

Despite being offhand Barfly was right, we couldn't afford to waste time drinking Cokes whenever we got hot, so we drained our glasses and went back into the heat for a spell of bike packing. Lots of little things needed fettling on the bikes after their transportation in the boxes. The tyres needed pumping up (they have to be deflated on a plane), the handlebars straightened, seats raised, and numerous other little tweaks. After about an hour we were finished and we stood back to admire our handy work. The once svelte machines now looked like fully burdened camels, and they gave me the impression that they would be just as cantankerous to manoeuvre.

Then came the gunshot. BANG!

'Shit, what the hell was that?' I asked.

'Christ I dunno,' came JK's startled reply.

Suspecting a potential skirmish at the border, Barfly had made his way to the doorway. Holding his beer and squinting out from the darkness he surveyed the scene. As his gaze reached us he crumpled his forehead disappointingly as if to say 'are you still here?'

'Oh shit, it's my back tyre.' JK moaned. He gave his bike another kick.

Realising the pseudo gunfire was down to the hapless limeys, Barfly shook his head in disdain and retired to his barstool. I couldn't believe it, our first puncture and we hadn't even started cycling. In order to fix the puncture JK's bike (aka Vick) needed to be upturned and of course this meant having to unpack everything. A usual ten minute puncture repair expanded into a half-hour debacle. It transpired that the cycle shop where JK had purchased his wheels had forgotten to put any rim tape on them (the rim tape prevents the inner tube from snagging on the rough spokes). The burst tube was irreparable and in one bang our spare tube cache had halved. As JK finished off his repacking I thought I would phone Wendy, my long suffering partner, and let her know we were about to set off. I knew she would be diligently waiting by the phone for news of my safety. The phone rang out unanswered.

We cycled the short distance from the bar to the checkpoint and set about taking the usual photographs. A young customs official asked if we wanted our picture taken on the Canadian side.

'I'll just ring Canada and check it is okay,' she said, and after a brief phone call she waved us through. In Canada we were greeted with an equally amiable young lady who obligingly took our picture. After she had retired to her station we stood astride our bikes and looked down the endless road ahead. Figuratively speaking, we were at the top of America and I pondered the enormity of the trip that lay ahead, and then turned to JK,

'Fuckin' A, this is it!'
It was dead on 12.00 noon.

Ouch, ouch, ouch, ouch, ouch, ouch went my knee during the first half dozen pedal strokes. And the next half dozen were very similar. But then things got a little better and it wasn't too long before the full blown ouches were relegated to slight winces, and then after a couple of miles I became aware that my knee wasn't hurting at all. It seemed too good to be true, but I wasn't complaining, I was more than happy to ride this pain free wave all to the way to the beach.

Of course the pain may have lessened because I was doped up to the eyeballs with vitamin I, our appellation for Ibuprofen, or because the pain signals were competing with those sent from my decaffeinated headache, or the discomfort from the unbearable heat. But it didn't matter, whichever way you look at it my knee didn't hurt and that was good news. Nonetheless the cacophony of general hurt and discomfort needed abating, and the intuitive tonic for these symptoms was an ice cold Coke. Ten miles later we entered the small town of Eureka – the self-proclaimed "Christmas Tree Capital of the World". Not surprisingly, in this heat Christmas was the furthest thing from my mind, right up there at the front of the queue was my ice-cold beverage. As we approached a mercantile I signalled to JK that I was slowing down and shouted over my shoulder that a Coke was in order. I pulled up outside the shop and started to dismount.
'You guys come far?' came a voice, not dissimilar to Barfly's, from a shaded bench on the porch.
Like déjà vu the fraudster feeling swept over me and without acknowledging the voice I cocked my leg back over Corsair and pedalled away leaving a bemused JK in my wake. Several hundred yards down the road and safely out of range of the voice, I pulled into a more anonymous looking gas station and purchased a couple of cold drinks, this time without question or remorse.

We continued for several miles through the Tobacco Valley, so called because of the tobacco crops the indigenous Kootenai Indians used to grow there, or more plausibly after the failed attempts of missionaries to grow the same plant. The reason I favour the latter is because the climate is not favourable for growing tobacco, nor (as I was learning rapidly) is it favourable for bike packing. Annoyingly the route swung through over ninety degrees and we pedalled up the inauspiciously named Grave Creek Road on a Northeast bearing. So much for heading south. After a further twenty miles we finally left the blacktop behind and in doing so started our off-road journey proper.

The change of terrain coincided with a sharp increase in gradient and a drastic reduction in speed. The trail meandered its way up through Kootenai National Forest, yet despite the abundance of trees there was very little shade due to the high position of the sun. We crawled our way at a little over two miles per hour through a five hour baptism by fire. Many years ago, when I was an undergraduate, I was involved in experiments determining the effects of heat and dehydration on human performance. To induce sufficient dehydration on the subjects they were required to cycle on a stationary bike inside a heat chamber whilst wearing non-breathable rubber suits. In addition they had to endure the experiment whilst a rectal thermometer was measuring their core temperature. Naturally volunteers weren't forthcoming despite my best hard-sell approach, and as such I often had to fill in and be a subject myself. They were not pleasant times. My main recollection of this period is experiencing the feeling of becoming cold despite knowing I was hot. This dichotomy usually occurred just before I collapsed.

Things were very similar on the trail if you substitute Corsair for the stationary bike, the sun for the heat chamber, and my saddle for the rectal thermometer. I also felt cold and shivery. Fortunately I became aware of this before it was too late and signalled to JK that I needed to stop. Not surprisingly he put up no resistance. We sat under the shade of a few trees in an attempt to help our bodies re-establish some kind of homeostasis.

'Jesus this is hot,' JK exhaled.

'I know, I'm going to have to get this mop cut off before I fry,' I said, eyeing up JK pouring water on his baldhead like Colonel Kurtz in Apocalypse Now.

'Do you want my two pennies worth?' he asked.

'Fire away.'

'You should have got it shaved before we left,' he smirked.

The net trend was up, but the climb became increasingly punctuated with short, sharp descents. These provided us with a much needed respite from the heat; the lack of pedalling and the increased wind speed meant we had a chance to cool down. It also helped with our average speed, we had been climbing for several hours and had only covered about four miles, at this rate the whole route was going to take years not weeks. At our next cool-down stop, JK got the main map out and we spread it on the ground. I was relieved to find out that the climb was going to top out shortly and there was an open camp ground in about five miles. The trail notes lifted my spirits somewhat and I read aloud the description.

'Crest Whitefish Divide - glorious descent through wild country,' and then noticed the warning, 'Watch out for grizzly bears!'

With regard to the former, the trail notes weren't wrong, the descent was awesome and we got some payback for our earlier climb. Fortunately with regard to the latter, there was no sign. The decline was particularly steep and as such we were forced to use our brakes a lot. After about fifteen minutes I could smell Corsair's rubber brake pads heating up. With hindsight I should have stopped and let them cool down, but to a mountain biker fresh out of Britain, where overheating rims are unheard of, it never crossed my mind. Then my rear wheel went sloppy and I could feel every rock that I rode over. I had punctured. The brake pads had heated up the rim of my wheel to such an extent that it caused the inner tube to blow. Rather than unpack Corsair, we managed to upturn him so that I could access the rear wheel. The process wasn't too difficult and was far simpler than stripping and repacking the load. As ever we turned every stop into a refection break and as I fixed my puncture I had a half melted Snickers bar hanging like a precarious cigarette out of the corner of my mouth. I swapped my blown tube with our remaining spare and while I was refitting the tyre I heard some movement in the trees behind me. I turned to look, but I couldn't see the perpetrator. Suddenly I became aware that my bike was not operational and I was covered in chocolate, an easy and inviting meal for a grizzly. I also noticed, out of the corner of my eye, that JK had mounted his bike and was poised like a competitor at the start of a race waiting for the gun. I refitted the tyre in double quick speed and hot-tailed it down the descent. Not surprisingly I didn't touch my brakes this time.

Shortly afterwards we arrived at Tuchuck open campground with 43 miles on the odometer. At the entrance was an inauspicious welcome sign, it read: 'THIS IS BEAR COUNTRY.' I put the warning to the back of mind as I looked for the positive aspects of my residence for the night. Although the campsite was primitive, there was flat ground between the trees, a few picnic tables, a toilet and a nearby stream. It was pretty much everything we needed. A little over-paranoid about bear attacks we ate our tea a few hundred yards away from our tent and got into the prudent habit of storing our food cache up a tree.

JK retired to the tent leaving me to give Corsair a once over, a slight creaking had developed during the day's ride and I was determined to locate it. Unfortunately, this was not to be. Frustrated and beaten by the recalcitrant creak, I propped Corsair up against a nearby tree and decided to call it a night. I stood next to our miniscule Vango two man tent, brushing my teeth and admiring the locale. JK's voice came from within the tent warning me that there was a break in protocol regarding the sleeping arrangements for the night.

'Oh Christ,' I muttered, 'what is it this time?'

His comment reminded me of a different camping experience we had shared. It was the previous year and we had just finished riding the South Downs Way. After overindulging during an en route café stop, JK had found the last section particularly tough. Upon returning to our campsite, he had immediately dived into the tent and fallen asleep. I had decided to take a stroll into the city in search of food. Upon my return I heard JK's meek voice.

'I'm sorry mate but I've had a couple of little accidents whilst you were away.'

Understandably, due to the tetchy nature of JK's digestive tract, a whole host of abhorrent thoughts ran through my mind as to what could have happened.

My initial response was: 'Is my sleeping bag okay?'

'Kind of,' came the apologetic reply.

As I unzipped the flysheet, JK's indiscretions became immediately apparent; he had regurgitated two neat piles of vomit towards the rear of the tent, and he had filled the inside with a particularly pungent strain of methane. Of course that night was not a good camp.

Fearing the worst for my present predicament, I pleaded, 'tell me you've not puked.'

'No, no, it is nothing like that,' he said reassuringly, then added, 'I'm going to have to go naked, it's like a sauna in here.'

Sure enough it was, and being naked was the furthest inconvenience from our minds, we had to deal with the infuriating paradox that we found ourselves in. If we opened the door in an attempt to reduce the temperature from searing to a mere boiling, the tent became infested with mosquitoes, whereas if we closed the door the insects were kept at bay but we cooked.

I spent the restless night pondering my predicament. Despite my best efforts to be upbeat I somehow allowed a degree of negativity to enter my thoughts, and once it was in there it ate through my morale with the callousness of a cancer. Earlier that day I had suffered like a dog on a ten mile climb that topped out at just over five thousand feet. Normally this would be a relatively good achievement, but the fact of the matter remained that later on in the journey I would have to climb a more severe route over Indiana Pass that was a whisker under twelve thousand feet, which for all intents and purposes is high altitude and so comes equipped with the debilitating effects worthy of the status. The sums were an additional problem, and no matter how I tried to mentally cook the books they just didn't add up. After our literal baptism by fire I honestly knew I had given it my all and there was no way I could have done any more. Yet the day's meagre forty two mile offering didn't even make a dent in the total, we still had two thousand four hundred and twenty eight miles to do instead of the initial two thousand four hundred and seventy. At this rate it was going to take us about nine weeks to complete the route, which was impracticable as we both had a plane to catch and jobs to return to after just six weeks. As far as I could see the whole fiasco was doomed. Despite being fully aware that I had jetlag and that I wasn't acclimatised to the heat yet, I still didn't give myself a break. To make matters worse, my long-term memory uncharacteristically kicked in and reminded me that, even though it was at the opposing end of the thermometer, this was how I felt when I competed in the IditaSport - an ultraendurance mountain bike race in Alaska. It also added that it's prognosis, based on my past performance, was that it was going to get worse. A lot worse.

The temperature must have dropped sometime after 4.00 am because that was the last time I remember looking at my watch. I managed to get a couple of hours of fitful sleep before JK's watch alarm went off at 6.00 am, signalling the start of our shift. Apparently JK had experienced a similar night and as we silently ate our trail mix breakfast the mood in the camp wasn't too good. We filled our Camelbak water bladders and our bidons at the nearby stream and treated them with iodine to make them drinkable. We shuffled a few of the items around on the bikes to make them more accessible and better weighted and then set off.

We cycled for about half an hour in our own silent worlds, each of us trying to rationalise our situation. Then it dawned on me, my knee wasn't hurting and I hadn't taken any vitamin I. I lifted my gaze from my hypnotic, cyclical front tyre and smiled to myself, my biggest problem was no more. The act of lifting my forehead off my bar bag also improved my disposition, I looked over my right shoulder at the path we had just ridden along and the scenery was truly awesome. I stood on pedals and closed the fifty yard gap that had opened up between JK and myself and pulled alongside him.

'It took a while to get into the rhythm back there,' I said enthusiastically, 'but now I feel great. This is unbelievable what we're doing.'

JK gave me a sideways glance, he was clearly suffering. 'Don't rub it in,' he muttered between gasps.

At times like this you have to deal with your own demons, there's nothing anyone can say or do to help. In fact it is pretty difficult to help without being patronising, so I left JK to overcome his hurdles alone and I pushed on up the trail. I desperately wanted to head south, but I was cycling directly into the morning sun and unless there had been a planetary shift during the last few days it meant that we were heading due east. The start of the route was overtly circuitous, which didn't mix well with my callow enthusiasm, but a map reference allayed my anxieties as it showed another ninety degree kink was coming up, affording us a full ten miles in a southerly direction. Not much, but every little counts.

The southerly section parallels the North Fork Flathead River which itself pretty much skirts the boundary of Glacier National Park. Fortunately the stunning scenery helped revitalise JK's flagging moral and he pulled up alongside me as I climbed up through the picturesque forest of lodgepole pine, ancient ponderosa pine and western larch.

'It's tough, but worth it,' he breathed.

'And you wouldn't have it any other way,' I replied enthusiastically.

In 1806, the Lewis and Clark Expedition ventured within 50 miles of what is now Glacier National Park. However, according to recent archaeological surveys, the Corps of Discovery were not the first people to set foot in this beautiful region. Apparently humans have roamed these parts for the last ten millennia and it is hypothesised that they may have been the ancestors of the more contemporary tribes that lived in the area. In the early days this region was home to several tribes; the Blackfeet Indians who inhabited the vast eastern prairies; and the Salish and Kootenai Indians who occupied the western valleys. But, in the early 1800s European trappers explored the area and brought with them an influx of settlers who forced the Indians onto reservations despite the area having great spiritual significance to the Indian people. Nowadays the area is a designated national park and residing within the protected 1,000,000-acre boundary are, forests, alpine meadows and lakes as well as scores of mammalian and literally hundreds of birds species.

As we pushed on, we passed through the remnants of Red Bench Fire – a massive forest fire that had savaged nearly forty thousand acres of this stunning vegetation back in 1988. The dead, skeletal trees are a reminder of the devastation that forest fires can bring, but the young fireweed and conifers that are sprouting out of the potash bring with them a new generation of hope for the future. After a few more miles of climbing we topped out at Red Meadow Lake. This really was a "chocolate-box" countryside vista; a pristine mirror lake edged with pine trees and a smattering of appropriately placed mountains. The air was still and there wasn't a sound to be heard, that is of course discounting the creaking Corsair was making. The creaking, as if protesting about the last climb, had developed from an irksome creakette into a fully fledged intrusive creak. Had this happened to my car, I would simply turn the stereo up to mask the issue - problem solved. But here in this tranquil setting it seemed to be magnified. Sort of like when you try and creep up the stairs after a late night out and the floorboards reveal your every move. I reasoned that it was the quiet surroundings that were the problem and that Corsair hadn't got any worse. Nonetheless, being a prudent bike packer who believes in preventative maintenance, I squirted some oil in the general direction of the bothersome noise.

It would have been ideal to spend a little more time at Red Meadow Lake, indeed to camp there – as the trail notes suggest – would have been perfect, but it was only midday and despite the heat we had too many miles to cover for this to be a reality. So we pedalled on. The pedalling soon gave way to coasting as the ride into Whitefish is mostly downhill and the miles quickly slipped by under our buzzing tyres. As we flew through Stillwater State Forest I signalled to JK that I was slowing down and pulled up next to a natural forest clearing that was brimming with flowers, herbs and shrubs.

'I've got to get a photo of this clearing,' I said to JK as he pulled up alongside me, 'the colours are really vivid, they should come out really well.'

I propped my bike up on a log in the foreground and set about composing my "award winning" shot.

'It says here,' said JK reading from the trail notes, 'that these clearings with their herbs and berries are favourite dining sites for grizzlies…'

I noticed that JK's voice was trailing off and I looked up from my viewfinder to see him riding off.

'I'll see you at the bottom,' he added.

Shit! I wasn't sure if he was being serious about the grizzlies or not, nonetheless I quickly took the photograph, with less care about the composition this time, and hurriedly followed JK's tracks whilst trying to appear nonchalant.

I caught up with JK on the final ride into Whitefish which was on paved road and we cruised two abreast. We had covered sixty miles and that put us into triple figures on the odometer. That if nothing else was worth celebrating, so we decided to treat ourselves to Whitefish's finest food.

CHAPTER THREE. WHITEFISH TO OVANDO

'you tend to carry your insecurities'

By Great Divide standards, Whitefish is a big town. It has a population of around four and a half thousand, many of whom are involved in the two main industries: logging and skiing. We'd seen plenty of evidence of the former as we had ridden through the forests, but in this heat it is difficult to imagine the place as a ski resort. That said, silently waiting for the snow to fall is the omnipresent Big Mountain, it looms above Whitefish and has drawn skiers to the area for over fifty years. However, it wasn't snow that had drawn me back to Whitefish on this midsummer's afternoon, it was the symbol on our map, a star. Translated it means Whitefish has full services, or more importantly: burritos, beds and inner tubes. And not necessarily in that order.

Despite protestations from my stomach, our first port of call was Glacier Cyclery in order to replenish our inner tube cache before the shop closed. JK went inside to purchase the tubes and cross off one of the items on our three item shopping list. I stayed outside and looked after the bikes. As I sat in the shade of the shop doorway, I noticed a sign out of the corner of my eye, it had the word hostel written vertically and the word burritos underneath. Without moving a muscle I was able to cross items two and three off the list as well. The hostel was called The Non-Hostile Hostel and sure enough there was no hostility to be found. Indeed the staff were hospitality personified, to such an extent that they allowed us to keep our bikes indoors. Already propped up in the entranceway was a behemoth mountain bike - a retro Cannondale circa 1994, kitted out with front and rear panniers and a burdened trailer. As we pushed our bikes past this colossus I was amazed by the amount of stuff the owner was hauling.

'Is that a track pump, in the trailer?' I asked JK,

'What, under the cast iron frying pan?' he sarcastically replied.

When I competed in the IditaSport race in Alaska, a fellow, and far more experienced, competitor looked at my overloaded bike and commented 'when packing for your trip, you tend to carry your insecurities.' Judging by the bike in the entranceway the rider must be neurotic.

We leaned our bikes next to the Cannondale and headed for the lounge-cum-café area. We each pulled up a barstool and ordered a burrito and a decaf. There were a few travellers milling around in the arty-decorated lounge area and one of the guys stood out as the owner of the Cannondale. He was about five foot ten, weighed about ten and half stone and had a wiry build. His longish hair was uncombed and he had a strange disconnected stare. Somehow he just went with the bike.

'Is that your 'Dale?' I asked

There was a slight pause, as if we were communicating via satellite, then

'Yep, sure is.'

'Where are you riding?' I quizzed.

Pause.

'Oh, I'm riding the Great Divide.'

Surely he couldn't look so trail hardened with just a hundred miles under his belt? JK and I just looked plain knackered, this guy had the thousand yard stare, he looked the part. I assumed he must have started further up in Canada.

'Where did you start?' I asked.

Pause.

'Mexico,' came his reply.

That explains it, and the fact that he was riding contra to the trail notes just added to the eccentricity.

'John Metcalfe,' I said extending my right hand.

'Monty,' he replied shaking it.

Monty was from Arizona, was a nurse by trade and was far from neurotic. He had saved up enough annual leave to do the Great Divide, but somewhere along the line red tape had got in the way and his employers wouldn't let him have all of his leave in one go. So with a panache that's hard to find these days he quit and started the ride anyway. He was an enthralling guy and we chatted for a while over coffee.

Later on that evening I ventured out in search of a barbers and even at this time of the day the heat was overwhelming. After wandering around for a few blocks I came across the aptly named Clip Joint. It was a one-woman show and due to her not being in a hurry, a relatively long queue had formed. As I walked in, all eyes turned to look at me and it reminded me of a scene from American Werewolf in London. I became self-conscious that I was wearing Lycra; such are the indiscretions of travelling light, I bet Monty had a change of clothes for every occasion packed away in his trailer. On the bike Lycra looks okay, although others may disagree, but without a bike in sight it looks odd at best and perverted at worst. I prayed they thought I was odd. After eyeing my attire, the woman shifted her gaze to my dreadlocks, raised her eyebrows and gave me a 'please don't ask me to tidy that up' glance. I sat myself down in the queue pretending that my Lycra outfit was no different to the jeans and check shirt uniform all of the other patrons were wearing and did what all other Englishmen do when faced with an uneasy social scene - I asked about the weather. I soon wished I hadn't. I learned that it had been a record breaking 107°F and that the papers were predicting that it was going to be broken again in the next few days.

Eventually it was my turn in the chair, and the hairdresser was visibly relieved when I told her I wanted a grade one. She fired up the clippers and mowed a single strip along the middle of my head. I looked at my inverse mohican in the mirror and prayed that there wasn't going to be a power cut. As she continued shearing my dreadlocked mop, we got onto the conversation about the Great Divide.

'How long will it take you?' she asked.

'Hopefully about six weeks,' I replied.

'There was a guy I went to see a couple of years ago just before he was making his record attempt,' she said stepping back from clipping my hair as she tried to think of his name.

Half my head was shaven and the other half unkempt. I was a real novelty in the Clip Joint that evening, a freak show haircut wearing Lycra.

'Was it John Stamstad?' I inquired in an attempt to get her back to work.

'That's right,' she said resuming clipping.

'What's he like?'

'Kinda laid back and hyperactive at the same time,' she said, and then added, 'do you know he drank canola oil while he was riding?'

'He drank what?' I quizzed.

'Canola oil,' she repeated, 'for the energy.'

Suddenly I felt at ease with my current dietary habits of eating a chocolate bar on the hour, every hour.

My new haircut made the heat more bearable and as I walked back to the hostel it was as though someone had turned the thermostat down a couple of degrees. Back at the digs we shuffled our gear around once again. What we thought was the perfect arrangement back in England proved impractical out on the trail. On Corsair I had a bar bag mounted on the handlebars that contains my personal items; sunglasses, snacks, camera, and our trail notes. Slung under the top tube, in a bright red Jandd frame bag was our workshop. It contained a multi-tool that can attend to most trailside repairs, inner tubes a couple of tyre levers, a mini pump and an assortment of nuts, bolts, cables and brake pads. On my rear rack was my wardrobe: a blue Ortlieb sausage bag containing a spare set of cycling wear, a sleeping bag and a duvet jacket. On top of that I had the tent, and any remaining stuff I put in my rucksack, which also housed a drinking bladder. JK had Vick kitted out in much the same way, except he had the field kitchen instead of the workshop. Our kitchen comprised an MSR Whisperlight stove, a one litre titanium pan, and a couple of titanium sporks (a spoon/fork hybrid). Basically we were travelling pretty light.

We were sharing a room with Monty who only had a couple of days of riding left and he was preparing for re-entry into civilisation after two months on the trail. He was a source of fresh trail knowledge, and informed us that the riding was good, but the weather was hot, very hot, and that later on in the ride finding water may become a problem. On that note we decided that an early start would be a prudent move so that we could avoid the midday heat. JK set the alarm for 5:00 am and we retired to our bunks. At some point during the night, the fourth person in our room, a rather large drunkard, came crashing through the door waking me (and I suspect JK and Monty) up in the process. He rambled around the room for ages and even when he found his bed he still disturbed the peace. I lay awake in my bunk, knowing that I had to go to sleep due to the early start. But the more I thought about it the less chance I had of making it a reality. I resigned myself to the notion that I was at the receiving end of a sleep deprivation conspiracy. At some point I eventually nodded off.

After a simple breakfast of Fig Newtons and orange juice, we headed out the door accompanied by Monty.
'I had to see you guys off,' he said, but I suspected he didn't want to be alone in the room with the drunkard, I know I wouldn't. He then sincerely added, 'take care and enjoy yourselves.'
Because the trail notes warned that there wouldn't be anywhere to buy food for a couple of days we were fully loaded with groceries, mainly chocolate bars, cereal bars, Fig Newtons and dehydrated meals. At the start of the day my rucksack was always at its heaviest, it is crammed with trail snacks and the water bladders and bidons are at their fullest. As I swung the sack onto my back it felt as though a small man had pressed his knees between my shoulder blades and was pulling back with his hands on my shoulders. I eased myself onto my saddle and winced, even a double dose of vitamin I and nappy cream couldn't prevent the white pain stemming from my arse.

The morning air was pleasantly cold which enabled us to make good headway, we cruised for several hours at a positively swift nineteen miles per hour. Mercifully the terrain out of Whitefish was relatively flat, but it unfortunately followed an infuriating series of right angles, which skirted farmers' land and denied us the shorter hypotenuse. The morning was pretty much uneventful and I had to amuse myself by trying to think of pop songs that fitted in to the crickety-creak backing beat that was emanating from Corsair's bottom bracket area. Crickety-creak? It was only a creak yesterday. I pulled over and checked out Corsair's nether regions, somehow the crank bolts had worked loose, so I gave them a tighten with an allen key and the creaking was silenced.

We'd got forty five easy miles under our belts by midday, so we pulled up under the shade of a tree at the side of the trail for a siesta. It was my time to play at Colonel Kurtz – I poured cold creek water over my shaven head and boy did it feel good. I rolled out my sleeping mat and instantly fell asleep. About five minutes later JK woke me up.

'We're going to have to get moving,' he said, 'the mossies are killing me.'

'Just give me half an hour mate, I need some kip,' I protested.

But there was no talking him round, JK was not in a good mood. There were several things that were annoying him today; in addition to the heat, the lack of sleep, and the mosquitoes, his rucksack was ill-fitting and he had developed an unusual and painful looking sore on the instep of his left foot. I yielded to his request, and in a state of sleep deprivation we cycled on.

We stopped at the foot of a six mile climb and had a map reference – cum – Snickers break – cum – piss stop. We were procrastinating because the climb looked like a tough bastard and the temperature must have been a hundred plus. We filled our drinking bladders at a nearby stream as much for a delay as for the water and then set about the inevitable task of climbing this six miler. On climbs like this our average speed can drop as low as two miles per hour and we would greatly increase the distance by zigzagging our way up following the contours of the climb. Another habit that seemed to have developed was to follow the shadows of the trees. As the trail meandered up the mountain the shadows fell on opposite sides of the trail and we hugged these little respites as if our lives depended on them.

No hill can go on forever and eventually we topped out at just over five thousand feet. Of course, what goes up must come down and as such we had an exhilarating six mile descent along pristine forest tracks. For over ten minutes I didn't have to pedal, but when I did the creaking had returned, only now it was more of a crickety-crickety-creak; an extra crickety had joined the chorus. Once again the recalcitrant noise ceded to the allen key, but it didn't bode well.

It was mid afternoon when we realised that we were lost. We had covered over seventy faultless miles on excellent logging tracks without cause for concern. But we had missed one of our earlier snack stops and as a result had become fatigued and had misread the map. That said the cartography of the trail maps leave a lot to be desired; think of an Ordinance Survey map and then take off all of the detail and you pretty much have it. We stopped at the junction of about five logging roads, with each one being plausible as our route.

The best thing to do in a situation like this is make something of the predicament. This was a trick I had learned when I was a spectator at a mountain bike race. Like all spectators with a morbid curiosity I had positioned myself at the most dangerous place on the course, the section where there would be the most crashes. It wasn't long before a hapless rider fell foul of the course and crashed in spectacular style. The crowd 'ooohhhed' and 'ahhhrrrddd' as he slowly ground to a halt on his arse. Staying remarkably collected, he casually reached out and plucked his water bottle from his nearby bike, turned to the baying crowd and said, 'I might as well have a drink while I'm here.'

With this worry-free philosophy in mind I reached into my bar bag and produced a box of Fig Newtons. As we steadfastly munched our way through the packet a distant rumbling became louder, fortunately it wasn't JK's gastro-intestinal tract, but a logging truck pulling into view. We flagged down the driver and asked him for directions. Ten minutes later we were back on the route with the added bonus of being fed and watered. We had now reached ninety odd miles and we figured it was a good time to call it a day. We dropped down onto State Highway 83, otherwise known as Swan Highway, and headed for a small hamlet called Condon. On the way Corsair's crank repeatedly worked loose and I had to pull over several times and tighten it up.

The cranks attach onto the bottom bracket (axle) with a splined fit; the protrusions of the bottom bracket are fluted which fit perfectly into fluted depressions in the crank arms. They are then held securely in place by the crank bolts. When the bolts initially became loose it meant that the cranks could wiggle ever so slightly on the bottom bracket axle. Because the cranks are made of relatively soft aluminium they must have become slightly deformed. This meant that even though I tightened them up the fit was no longer perfect and therefore they quickly worked loose and the process repeated itself. The situation was only going to get progressively worse. Of course my cranks were playing up when we were a hundred miles from Glacier Cyclery in Montana, and over one hundred and sixty miles away from the next bike shop in Helena. Faced with such a situation, and being an adroit mechanic, I left Corsair to the overnight fairies and headed straight for Chuck's Bar.

Chuck's Bar was great, it was dark, smoky, had cowboys playing pool, cowgirls who loved English accents and served steaks the size of cows. There was kind of a cow-theme to it. We pulled up a couple of barstools and each ordered a Chuck Steak with salad. Seeing my reflection in the mirror behind the bar I again became aware that I was wearing Lycra in a public place. Obviously there were now two of us and I wasn't sure if that was a good or a bad thing. The locals didn't seem to mind one bit, they badgered us for travel stories and tales from England. We obliged and of course embellished and at precisely the right moment JK asked Chuck if he had some space in his land out the back for a couple of weary trailhounds to pitch their tent. Chuck gave us the thumbs up and after a great feed we bid our hosts goodnight and pitched our tent amongst the dumpsters and fatigued caravans in the yard at the back of the bar.

During the night the fairies hadn't bothered to touch Corsair, as the creaking was resonating with a vengeance the next morning. Because we were pretty much stuck equidistant between two towns we had no other option but to press on towards Helena and hope that the crank would hold up until then. Helena is about two days' riding from Condon and I was fairly confident that it would hold out providing I was vigilant and tightened it up every time we stopped for a map reference or a food break.

The morning ride was more of the same, a punch in the face from the heat, whilst being gently caressed by the scenery. The juxtaposition was a strange cocktail and it was proving difficult to determine whether I was enjoying it or not. The track we were following guided us through forests of beautiful western larch, which can grow up to two hundred feet, but after several hours of riding even these tall and impressively straight trees were becoming hackneyed. Fortunately there were regular clearings that afforded us views across the valley of the magnificent Swan Mountains to the east and Mission Mountains to the west. Although it somehow seemed impossible to be suffering in such majestic surroundings, we were. JK was in a pretty miserable frame of mind; he hadn't slept properly since we started, the heat and the mosquitoes were bugging him, the sore on his foot was getting worse, and to add insult to injury my creaking crank was pissing him off.

It was a tough morning of climbing, but the reward was good, the profile on the map showed a twenty mile downward slope that meanders around Richmond Peak into a spectacular alpine basin and eventually Seeley Lake. Seeley Lake was another highlight on the map as it was accompanied by a full services star and after a couple of days of figs and candy bars some real food was needed, and the sooner the better. The descent was fast, exhilarating and exceedingly technical in places. At times the trail was severely eroded and the route was very rocky, at other times it was overgrown and no obvious path was evident. At such a point we decided to have a map reference stop to check where we were.

'If we are where I think we are,' said JK fumbling around with the map, 'we're in a place called Grizzly Basin. 'It says that you should keep your eyes peeled for bears on the move through the avalanche chutes…'

Not wanting to hang around and taking a leaf from JK's own manual for self-preservation, I set off downhill towards Seeley Lake.

'I'll see you at the bottom' I said feeling rather smug that I had given him a taste of his own medicine. Touché. Then my front wheel washed out, I dabbed out my foot – which proved to be a feeble outrigger – and I ground to a halt in the undergrowth.

'Not unless I get there first!' I heard JK chortling as he zipped by.

Doh!

We took a two mile detour from the trail to get to Seeley Lake. It may only have a population of about eight hundred and seventy, but it does boast a supermarket with a pizzeria inside and a laundrette – a plush town by any bikepacker's standards. We devoured several large deluxe pizzas, numerous decafs and several Cokes, before we even thought about replenishing any other supplies. On our shopping list was, nappy cream, baby wipes, trail mix, noodles, dehydrated potatoes and cheese slices. We had decided to pass on the chocolate for a while because it was melting in the heat, instead we made up for it with extra Fig Newtons and cereal bars.

With our hunger satiated and our thirsts slaked, we waddled across the main road to the laundrette. It was our inaugural wash and my used clothes had been festering for a day or so in my sausage bag. The smell that emerged as I opened the bag can only be described as tramp-like and it immediately took me back to Seattle and the guy rummaging in the bins. The clothes I was standing up in weren't faring much better as I had been wearing them for a day and a half. So I stripped down to my cycling shorts and bunged everything in the washer. I rolled out my sleeping mat outside the laundrette in the shade of the eaves and tried to get some rest. JK was already sitting down outside tending to the growing sore on his foot. It now looked like a large piece of bubble wrap filled with a mixture of washing up liquid and chicken soup. We had a debate about the pros and cons of lancing it. Enthralled I fell asleep.

I woke with a startle as JK placed a cold can of Coke on my bare chest.

'We'd better make a move,' he said

'How long have I been asleep?' I groggily enquired, trying to open the can.

'About an hour,' he answered belching out Coke gas.

I was initially pissed off that he had woken me up, but it soon turned to guilt when I noticed that he had sorted out my laundry and packed up Corsair for me. JK was having a tough time at the moment, and at least I had managed to have a bit of kip.

We saddled up and set off, skirting the southern edge of an excellently named Scapegoat Wilderness Area. How it came by this name I don't know, and to be honest I don't know whether I want to. The terrain was pretty easygoing, mainly on dusty gravel roads, but we felt tired and fatigued nonetheless. After about twenty five miles we encountered Ovando, a nice backwater hamlet and decided to call it a day. We had ridden nearly seventy miles giving us an odometer reading of two hundred and sixty three. We cruised into the village square which was home to a flagpole that proudly flew the stars and stripes. The square was framed by a mercantile, a museum, a trading post and an angling store. The wooden buildings were straight out of a western movie, fancy wooded facades at the front with a shed-like structure behind. We coasted up to the mercantile first because it looked like it might sell food.

A middle-aged couple were sitting outside on chairs and welcomed us in to their family shop. They were a cheery, laidback couple who went out of their way to be helpful.

'You guys doing the bike route?' she asked.

'That's right,' I answered, and then inquired about a nearby campsite.

'Mmmm processed cheese,' JK said from deep within an isle.

'You can camp in front of the museum,' the man offered, craning his neck to see what JK was up to, 'that's where all of the other bikers camp up.'

'That'll be great,' I commented and pushed my luck at little further, 'are there any showering facilities nearby?'

'There's a pipe out the back, and she'll be happy to hose you down,' he said nodding towards his wife.

I wasn't sure what to say.

'How much does it cost?' JK questioned from over my right shoulder.

I was relieved to see that JK was holding up a small loaf of bread.

'He's only pulling your leg,' she said reassuringly after seeing my bemused face.

'I can't even get her to hose me down,' he said laughing.

JK staggered out from an isle with an armful of goodies.

'Did you say other bikers had come through?' JK asked.

'Yeah we've had a few through this year,' he said.

'Have you seen an English couple recently?'

'It's hard to say, there's been a few Europeans pass through and an Australian, but you all sound the same so it's difficult.'

The reason JK was asking about the English couple was because some friends of a friend were also riding the route this year. Their names were Rosie and Stuart and as they were aiming to complete the route in fourteen weeks, we were looking forward to catching them up.

We pitched the tent outside the Brand Bar Museum and cooked up a basic meat broth, followed by an invigorating hose down with ice cold water. Afterwards when we were just milling around the campsite, I noticed a character staggering across the road towards us with a few cans of Miller tucked under his arms. He leant on the corral fence that bordered the Museum, looked at us for a while and then drawled, 'you guys look like you could do with a beer.'

'Cheers,' I said and took a can off him. It was lukewarm – unnervingly about body temperature.

'Cheers,' said JK.

At this early point JK was quick to realise that this guy was the village idiot and as such he quickly busied himself elsewhere. I on the other hand hadn't twigged and so tried to engage him in conversation. He muttered the odd slurred word but much of our tête-à-tête was dominated by a pregnant pause. I broke the silence.

'So have you done any travelling?'

He looked me straight in the eyes and said nothing. I was about to say something else, when he started.

'I aint bin mower than fifteen miles thata way,' he drawled, pointing his can over his right shoulder. 'And I aint bin mower than fifteen miles thata way,' pointing his can over his left shoulder.

The penny dropped, I was dealing with a drunken fruitcake.

He suddenly added, 'of course I own the fucking place,' and in doing so shocked the both of us.

On that note I made my excuses and retired to my sleeping bag.

As per usual the sweltering heat rendered sleeping impossible and to make things even more uncomfortable I had developed an intolerable thirst. After an hour or two of lying prone I decided to fetch my water bottle from Corsair. Emerging from the tent I was unnerved to see the village idiot still propping up the fence even though it was now dark.

He silently watched me as I retrieved my water bottle and returned to the tent. I glanced over to him, but he didn't acknowledge me. To add to the fear factor, a dramatic thunderstorm was being staged in the distance behind him. Of course once in the tent I couldn't sleep because of the freak outside. A short while later the thunderstorm had moved up the valley and was now raging overhead. I felt a little more at ease, thinking that the violent rain would drive him back to where he had come from. Not surprisingly I didn't have the courage to check, just in case he was still there, as that would have really freaked me out.

CHAPTER FOUR: OVANDO TO BASIN

'it was becoming one humiliation after another'

JK is no oil painting, nor for that matter am I, but this morning JK looked particularly rough. His eyes were swollen due to the lack of sleep and his behaviour was somewhat subdued. Like a pair of muted robots we set about our daily routine of breaking camp and repacking the bikes. Each morning I'd had a little rush of excitement when we'd completed the packing and the bikes were ready to roll. The idea that moments earlier our shelter existed and now it was stowed away ready for another camp at an unknown destination always excited me – even on this jaded morning. Ovando was asleep when we set off. The crunching of our tyres and of course the omnipresent creaking were the only sounds to break the silence as we rode along the track leading out of the square. Our drunken friend was nowhere to be seen, but he must obviously be holed up somewhere within a fifteen mile radius.

The next two major towns on the trail were Lincoln and Helena, at thirty five and ninety eight miles respectively. Both are given a luxurious full services star on our trail map, yet full services means different things to different people. Bearing in mind we were using a cycling map, it is not unrealistic to assume that full services means that there would be all of the facilities you would need if you're cycling the route. In other words you would expect there to be a cycle shop. However, it seems that this is not always the interpretation of the cartographers, after phoning around it transpired that there was a bike shop in Helena, whereas in Lincoln there wasn't, even though they have been given the same status. So the bottom line was that we had just under one hundred miles to go before I could get Corsair's crank looked at. At a push we could do it in one day, but it would take so long the shop would probably be shut, what's more it was Sunday and there was a fair chance it would be closed anyway. Because of this we decided to do about seventy-ish miles, camp on the trail, then ride the remaining thirty in the morning, timing it so that we arrive when the shop opens.

The morning was cloudy, perhaps reflecting JK's mood, and as a result the sun was less harsh. This meant that one of our many stressors had been turned down slightly and we were able to get some relatively comfortable miles under our wheels. Indeed the release of pressure meant that we could actually talk whilst riding, which made the experience a lot more pleasurable. As ever, we stopped on the hour, every hour for a food break. It was only for about ten to fifteen minutes, but it made all of the

43

difference; if we forwent one we soon ground to a halt further down the trail. On our third stop, I heard the familiar metallic sound of a frustrated cyclist changing down through the gears. It wasn't long before a fellow mountain biker – and our first encounter with one – appeared from one of the many switchbacks we had just ridden up.

He pulled up alongside us.

'Hi, are you guys doing the Divide?' he huffed.

'Yeah, yourself?' I answered, then added, 'oh by the way I'm John and this is JK.'

'Patrick,' he said offering his hand, 'I'm just riding this section, I'm doing a bit each year. It's kinda difficult getting the time off work, although the riding has been so good so far I might just quit work altogether.'

Patrick wore a permanent enthusiastic beam and was an experienced rider from Idaho who knew a lot about riding in the heat. He offered us some hot weather riding tips and we swapped trail stories for a while. He amused me with a little anecdote from a few days back:

'...so there I was cruising down through the forest, wondering why they call it Grizzly Basin when I turned a corner and there was a bear right in the middle of the trail. It must have weighed about two hundred pounds plus. It seemed to take an age for me to stop,' he said tapping his bike which was fully laden with front and rear panniers 'and when I did, we just looked at each other for a while, and then he sloped off in to the trees. I now know why it's called Grizzly Basin!' he chortled.

Because we were travelling light and because Patrick was in no particular hurry we said our farewells and left him behind to enjoy the peace and solitude. It wasn't long before we pulled into Lincoln and as ever our stomachs took priority. We propped up the bikes in front of a quintessential roadside diner and headed inside. I ordered some scrambled eggs on toast and a decaf, then while they were being cooked I phoned Wendy, who I assumed would be fraught with worry about my safety. This time I got through.

'Hi Wends it's me,' I said in my best weary-traveller-cum-tough-guy voice. I was a little disconcerted by the background noise.

'I'm sorry John, you'll have to speak up; I'm having a party...'

So much for the distraught loved one desperate for news of my progress.

The eggs and toast didn't stay on my plate for long, so I ordered extra toast and some hash browns. I probably overate, but it seemed to do the trick. We sat for a while and discussed our plans whilst drinking the endless supply of coffee refills. As we were doing so Patrick cycled passed the window; he was making good ground considering he was carrying a lot of gear. This galvanised JK into action, who has a competitive streak a mile wide running through him. He took a big swig of his coffee and hurriedly started getting himself ready. I had run out of water, so I asked a rather attractive young waitress if she could fill up my water supplies. She agreed. I then produced my drinking bladder which had been stained an appropriate urine colour by the iodine I had been using to purify the water. To all intents and purposes it looked like a colostomy bag. I tried to reassure her that it wasn't but I'm not sure she believed me. She screwed up her face and held it at arms length between her finger and thumb and ran through to the back.

JK threw me his.

'Get her to fill that up as well, could you?'

It was becoming one humiliation after another.

The climb out of Lincoln was to be a first, it was our introductory crossing of the Continental Divide. We pedalled for fifteen, hard, drawn out miles up the west flank of the Rockies before crossing over to the east side. The fanfare wasn't there, nor were the dancing girls, indeed it was a rather inauspicious moment. A lot of this area has been scarred by the greed of so-called civilisation; it was over logged, over mined and overrun with forest roads. Nonetheless that was one crossing of the Continental Divide in the bag, only twenty six more to go. The second crossing was already on the horizon eighteen miles away. The topography in between was a nine mile descent, losing almost two thousand feet, followed by a nine mile climb regaining most of the altitude. But once we had made it back up the geography was a steady ridge for fifteen miles to crossing number three at Priest Pass. We crested the Pass and with that we clocked off for the day. We had put in seventy miles on roller coaster terrain and were pretty knackered. We made camp near a stream called Dog Creek and tucked into a bland supper of dehydrated potatoes and water. No Michelin stars today.

**

The twenty five mile morning ride in to Helena was easy, mainly because it was all downhill. It was also one of the most interesting being littered with derelict mines and having a fascinating history. As we rode away from our camp we were following in the tyre tracks laid down by the 25th Infantry Bicycle Corps who on June 16th 1897 made their way to Fort William Henry Harrison, Helena. The 25th Infantry was a black Indian armed regiment formed by the Army as a result of the Civil War. They became famously known as the Buffalo Soldiers, a sobriquet given to them by the Indians they were sent to suppress. Lieutenant James A. Moss, one of the regiment's white officers, was an advocate of the bicycle and purportedly wrote:

'The bicycle has a number of advantages over the horse – it does not require much care [WRONG!]…it is noiseless [WRONG!] and raises little dust [WRONG!] and it's impossible to tell direction from its tracks.'

Those are my conflicting brackets, but of course I agree with the Lieutenant's last comment, indeed at times I have found it impossible to tell a bicycle's direction even when I'm riding it. The Lieutenant was so enthusiastic about two-wheeled, human powered transport, that he organised a one thousand nine hundred mile expedition ride from Fort Missoula to St. Louis. Kitted out with Spalding bicycles, balloon tyres and panniers, Moss and twenty of his troops set forth into the wilderness. During their forty one days in the saddle, the 25th Infantry faced similar hardships to those that I had faced; mosquito infestations, thunder storms, and debilitating heat amongst other nasties. And what's more they did it on bikes that only had one gear; why is it there's always one smart arse that is prepared to piss on your chips, even before you've started?

Formerly known as Last Chance Gulch, Helena was a major gold-rush mining area in the mid-1800s. But unlike countless other Montana gold funded cities, Last Chance Gulch avoided relegation to ghost town status when the gold boom dried up in 1866. Changing mining techniques and long-term planning are credited for its prosperity, to such an extent that when Montana became the forty first state, Helena had more millionaires per capita than anywhere else in the country. These days Helena has a population of over twenty four and a half thousand, and to my questionable gastronomic delight, it also had a McDonald's. Well, I had been eating some pretty dire food for the past few days. With my breakfast McMuffin and shake vaporising in my stomach, we cycled through the hot streets in search of the bike shop.

Over the last one hundred miles I had got my head around the worst prognosis for Corsair's crank – and my wallet – that it would have to be replaced. This was particularly grating because having bought a new set for the Great Divide they were practically unused. However, I managed to remain pragmatic: for years I had viewed the advertisements in American mountain bike magazines with a mixture of annoyance and envy. It seemed that there was a huge price difference between US and UK prices for components. The only exchange rate it seemed was to substitute the dollar sign for a pound sign. Or put another way we were paying about an extra third back in the UK. So,

I reasoned that if a component needed replacing America was the best place for it. Oh, how we tell ourselves the best of lies.

The bike shop was pretty easy to locate and looked promising because it had a comprehensive range of mountain bike equipment. I explained my predicament to a sales woman who, on first appraisal, seemed sincere, friendly and helpful. Of course, never one to miss an opportunity to build up his part, JK busied himself telling embellished Great Divide stories to any unsuspecting customers who would listen.

'If you just take it through to Steve, the mechanic, he'll sort it out,' she said pointing towards the rear of the shop.

I don't know if you've ever had an encounter with a British mountain bike mechanic, but they tend to be misanthropic at best. They're not out to win any popularity contests, but on the whole they are good at their chosen vocation. In England I treat my local grease monkey with a respectful prudence even though I have known him for over five years. To me, a mountain bike mechanic is like a pit bull; I get very wary when I'm near one, even if I know it has never done anyone any harm. There is something a little loose-cannonish about them. To walk straight in to the workshop and ask an unknown mechanic for a favour seemed like folly to me. Yet to my astonishment, as I approached the lion's den, the floorboards weren't reverberating to the thumping sound of The Prodigy, nor was there clanging of metal punctuated with profanity. Comforting, but I wasn't going to let my guard down.

'Steve?' I timidly inquired.

'Yep,' he replied straightening himself up. He returned the spanner he was holding to an anal-neat shadow board and rubbed his hand on his apron.

'Hi, I'm John,' I offered.

'Hi,' he replied extending his cleaned hand, 'what can I do for you?'

Taken aback by the lack of tattoos, body piercing and general aloofness, I responded, 'erm, I think the cranks have gone. Could you have a look at them, and if they're knackered could you replace them?' I was caught off guard by the pleasant ambiance, and put all of my cards on the table.

'I'll just pop it on the stand and give it the once over,' he said wheeling Corsair up to the slab, 'you have a look around the shop if you want, I'll bring it out when I'm finished.'

'Thanks Steve.'

'You're welcome.'

I chatted to the sales woman for a short while with the intention of charming her with tails of the trail so that she might offer me a discount. In lightening quick time – compared to my fellow country mechanics – Steve had finished and he wheeled Corsair up to the counter.

'That'll be one hundred and fifty dollars please,' the sales woman stated.

I pulled my credit card out of my wallet whilst simultaneously doing the maths – about one hundred quid.

'How much?' I retorted, pulling my card back.

'One hundred and fifty dollars,' she repeated slowly and added, 'and we're not charging for labour.'

Two months earlier I had purchased an identical crank for eighty pounds from a shop in the so-called expensive UK. It now appeared that the exchange rate was more like, replace the pound sign for a dollar sign and then double it. I became aware that I was over the proverbial barrel, what was I supposed to do? The next bike shop was seventy miles away.

The saleswoman wore a beaming smile; I smiled back and offered my credit card once more. As she took it from my grasp I heard myself give the Pavlovian English response 'thank you'. I was pissed off that I had said thanks. What was I thinking? I had just been ripped off, why was I thanking her? I got the formalities of signing the till roll out of the way, and I rolled Corsair out of the shop.

'Have a nice day.' I heard over my shoulder.

'Fuck you.' I said under my breath.

Back outside the temperature was doing its usual thing – soaring. We left the town of Helena and entered Helena National Forest via the ominously named Grizzly Gulch. Once again we avoided finding out why the gulch had earned its title and I hoped Patrick would be just as lucky this time. We now faced an eight mile climb, ascending almost two thousand vertical feet whilst the sun simultaneously climbed to its zenith. Almost immediately JK was suffering and the heat was really getting to him. The old sporting adage "there's no motivation quite like an opponent's suffering" came to mind, and my instinct was to up the ante and break JK on the climb. Whilst that kneejerk reaction would serve me well in a race, it was entirely futile, not to mention inhospitable, in the present situation. I really had to make a conscious effort to curtail my pace and my cheap desire to feed my ego. I glanced over my shoulder only to see him in a slumped riding position with his helmet slung over his handlebars – JK had obviously bonked. This doesn't mean that he'd had a fortuitous liaison with a young woman on one of the many switchbacks, rather it is the more dissonant situation of becoming hypoglycaemic

48

and fatigued. Bonking is the American term for running out of energy – or hitting the wall as it is referred to in running – and has become a British cycling colloquialism. It is an awful state to be in and it takes a strong mind to override the overwhelming desire to quit.

I had been in a race with JK several years earlier when he had bonked. On a particularly steep climb about two thirds into the race I saw JK grimacing and looking awful. When he pulled level he said he was going to quit at the next feed station and I tried in vain to talk him out of it. He was looking at me with one of those thousand yard stares and assured me that although I was his friend he would not hesitate to kill me if I made him continue. So we sat down and ate flapjacks. The transformation for JK was instantaneous and he was back on his bike pushing big gears in no time. However the flapjacks did not have the same ergogenic properties for me and it was all I could do to hang on to his wheel. There were times during the rest of the race when I wished he had pulled out.

With this in mind, I called an impromptu food break on the pretence that I was in need of some sustenance. Unfortunately it did nothing to revive JK, I think it was more of a heat problem than a fuel one this time. He drank copious amounts of water in a fashion that, given half the chance a slug covered in salt would. This seemed to help a bit, but he was definitely riding below par. Once again I was faced with the tricky situation of what to do, to offer encouragement or sympathy in these situations can often be regarded as condescending. So I figured I should do what I would have wanted JK to do if the roles were reversed. I dropped down a gear, stood on my pedals and left him alone to deal with his demons. It was getting close to lunch time when I stopped on one of the false summits of the day's laborious climb. I leant Corsair against a nearby tree and waited for JK. After about ten minutes he trudged in to view.

'Lunch time,' I said as he topped out.

In an amazingly fluid move, JK silently dismounted and rolled onto his back and exhaled like a burst Hoover bag. I removed the field kitchen from Vick and set about preparing a pre-packaged pasta meal. We cut ourselves a bit of slack and had a two hour lunch break, and when we finally set off the sky was clouding over. The temperature had dropped by a few degrees which was enough to revive JK and put a bit of verve back into his legs. I think he had something to prove (to himself more than to me) and his lead up the single-track climb called Lava Mountain Trail to the top of today's ascent was nothing short of a storming ride. The grade levelled off and we entered a beautiful meadow which was in full bloom. The juxtaposition from total discomfort on the climb to coasting through the meadow has never been more intense. Unfortunately, the harmony was short lived and storm clouds gathered overhead with alarming speed. Then it hailed. I was struck on my right shoulder by a hailstone the size of a golf ball. It was as if someone had thrown a rock at me. I grasped a handful of brake and dismounted, hopping around in pain whilst holding my shoulder. Then another hit in my chest, then another and another. Of course this had to happen when we were in an open meadow without shelter. I fumbled around in my sausage bag for extra clothes, as much for protection as for warmth.

The hail turned to rain which steadily increased in ferocity in tandem with our speed as we made our way down the mountain towards the small town of Basin. The rain was now reaching biblical proportions and JK got wind of a heavenly scent, a barbeque. With lightening quick reactions he darted through some trees, awkwardly slid across a wooded bridge and deposited himself just outside a log cabin to the astonishment of the occupants who were sitting on the sheltered veranda watching the storm. It was all I could do to follow his wheel. In fact it was more than I could do, for I indecorously slid up to the veranda on my arse. The residents, unperturbed by their impromptu guests, handed us steaming mugs of hot chocolate like it was an every day occurrence. We pulled up two chairs on the porch, whilst the rain hammered the tin roof and we chatted. It turned out that our hosts, David and Sarah were city slickers who were making a twelve hundred mile round trip just to spend a couple of days at the cabin. Once it became apparent that the rain wasn't abating and that drinking five cups of a stranger's hot chocolate was bordering on outstaying your welcome, we said our goodbyes. Looking forlornly at the barbeque I remounted Corsair and coasted down the mountain.

Half way down the descent JK spotted a neon sign in the valley, Merry Widow Motel. An ominous name for a guesthouse, but it will do for me. We splashed off the dirt track and on to the blacktop that lead to Basin and the Merry Widow. Basin is an ironic entrepreneurial town that makes a living drawing people who pay good money to visit an attraction that other people in the country pay good money to get rid of. The attraction is an old uranium mine where people converge to relax in the reputedly therapeutic atmosphere of low level radioactive radon gas. The gas is said to stimulate the pituitary gland and is heralded as benefiting maladies from migraines to lupus and everything between. It is the same gas that other residents of the Rockies have paid good money to have removed from their basements. Even Del-boy would be proud of that one. We checked in at the Merry Widow which was more of a recreational vehicle (RV) park, so it looked like it was another night under canvas. It was still raining pretty hard and the receptionist took pity on us,

'I can let you stay in the communal hall,' she said, 'provided you don't tell anyone.'

(I swore I wouldn't, and have kept this promise right up until I put finger to keyboard). The communal hall was a heated recreational area with a pool table, comfy sofas and a cooking area. In short it was ideal. We made ourselves scarce and headed into the centre of Basin to find that the only business still plying its trade at this time of night was a café. Some days things just go your way. I was having a seafood craving and I more than satiated it with a halibut steak with all the trimmings. We returned to the empty recreational area and promptly crashed out on the comfy, resplendent velour sofas.

CHAPTER FIVE. BASIN TO RED ROCK

'hardcore'

Apparently it takes about fourteen days to become acclimatised to the heat and we had been on the trail for seven days, so I guess we were half way there. Indeed things were feeling a lot easier as I cycled away from Basin towards Butte. I gave a knowing smile as I thought about the two naïve, alabaster cyclists setting off from the border one week ago. Dare I say it, I think they were even a little portly. Although I was not sporting the kind of tan you'd write home about, nor had the waistband on my shorts slackened, I would still like to think I had a week's experience under my belt and that my body had adapted and changed to suit the environment. And maybe, just maybe, I was turning into a cyclist. Of course the sceptics would point to the fact that the topography is flat for the thirty miles between Basin and Butte and that the morning cloud cover had relegated the temperature to the upper eighties. Choosing not to entertain this kind of tedious trivia and ignorantly buoyed by a placebo effect, I even deliberated whether I could make a dent on John Stamstad's record ride.

If the truth be known, it really is flat all of the way into Butte, despite a relatively low-lying fourth Continental Divide crossing. Butte is situated on the 'Richest Hill on Earth' and it began life in the 1860s first as a low level gold mine, and then as a silver mine the following decade. It wasn't until the late 1880s when, with the discovery of copper, Butte prospered. During the 'electrical revolution' of these times, copper became the new gold and as a result Butte grew into the largest copper producer in the world. In the second half of the last century the huge hill was further excavated and the earth was smelted for its precious metals, leaving Berkerley Pit – a staggeringly large hole that is over a mile wide and sixteen hundred feet deep. Since the mining stopped in 1982 the pit has been filling with toxic water that has seeped through the abandoned mines and has become a major concern for environmentalists. Surprisingly Berkerley Pit is one of the city's chief tourist attractions.

As interesting as this is, the main tourist attraction for me was the Cornish pasty dish that is served up at most of the restaurants and for some reason is heralded as the official food of Butte. Concerned about the blatant plagiarism of one of my country's best inventions, I set about getting to the bottom of this contemptible claim.

'Are you ready to order?' the waiter asked.

'Ahh, yes. I would like one of these pasties,' I said tapping the picture in the menu, whilst checking out his body language for any signs of guilt. I then added in my best detective manner, 'and can you perchance tell me how the pasty became the official food of Butte?'

'Yeah, one of the miners who worked here years ago used to live in Cornwall,' he replied, and then, a little too condescending for my liking, he added, 'they have pasties in Cornwall you know.'

Case unceremoniously solved.

Having replenished our supplies at the local supermarket, we set about our journey once more. The terrain was pretty much the same as on previous days and with my newfound cyclist's body I was actually able to enjoy the Montana climbs, and even have the general day-to-day awareness and presence of mind to be able to notice the little gofers that darted suicidally across the trail, just inches from my wheel. Lamentably, the enjoyment and enhanced physiology were ephemeral, and diminished as the grade steepened. As we climbed up to Continental Divide crossing number five my upright, beaming posture underwent an unbecoming metamorphosis, and in a reverse evolutionary manner I once again resumed my Neanderthal chin-on-the-handlebars position. As my sweat painfully leached into my eyes I cursed my pseudo-cyclist's body and could even sense John Stamstad's record slipping through my grasp.

As we crested the crossing, I was revived by a refreshing assault on my senses; we had entered a beautiful aspen park, which had an invigorating fragrance of sage and excellent views of the Pioneer Mountains in the west. It was a truly stunning location that made the toil of the climb pale in comparison to its beauty. But the best thing about the Continental Divide crossings is that they are the highest area of ground in the immediate vicinity, which means no pedalling and momentary free miles. The ensuing ten mile descent was fast, fun and technical, but as with all descents it became increasingly tarnished with the growing knowledge that a climb was imminent. However, over the last week I've learned that the only way for me to get my head around these things is to live in the here and now; I was on a descent and I was going to savour it – the climb would come soon enough. I was enjoying my time rattling down the breathtaking trail, just a few feet off JK's rear wheel, when he slammed on his brakes and slowly skidded to a halt. I instinctively peeled off to the right and did likewise.

'I don't believe it!' he shouted, looking skywards.

'What?' I quizzed.

'My crank is fucking loose!'

Sure enough JK's cranks had suffered the same fate as my old set. Vick and Corsair could really pick their moments. If I didn't know any better I'm sure they were doing this on purpose as some sort of militant protest against not being properly serviced. It goes without saying it couldn't have happened in Butte where there was a bike shop – that would have been too easy. We were now thirty miles away from Butte and there was of course the Continental Divide crossing in the way which meant climbing back up to nearly seven and a half thousand feet.

'It's your call,' I said, not relishing the thought of backtracking.

'There's only one option, we'll just have to push on,' he offered.

JK was right, to retrace our steps would take a day out of our schedule, which was already so tight that it was questionable whether we were going to make it anyhow. We cycled on for another seven or so miles and made camp at the first available place, Beaver Dam campground. By Great Divide standards this campsite was pretty plush; it had picnic benches, a toilet and even had a hand pump for drinking water.

With our camp set up, JK addressed Vick's problems with the resignation of a Lottery loser facing the realisation of a nine to five the following day. As he was helplessly prodding Vick's upturned carcass, a fellow camper wandered over and slapped two chilled bottles of Budweiser on our picnic table. Eager for an excuse to abandon Vick, JK downed tools and drained his Bud. Our temporary neighbour was Andy, a psychiatrist, who was spending a few days in the mountains with his wife Coni. Andy was an ex-climber and road cyclist, but more appropriately, in a former life, he was a tradesman. We promptly introduced him to Vick.

'Hmm,' he said contemplatively stroking his ponytail, 'have you heard of a Chicago fit?'

'A what?' asked JK.

'A Chicago fit. Basically you could hammer the crank onto the bottom bracket,' he explained.

Now this is my kind of maintenance and best of all I couldn't believe that someone had had the impudence – or panache – to give it a proper name.

'The metal in the crank will deform around the bottom bracket,' he added, 'and will mould itself to it. It will stay on for sure, but you'll never be able to get it off again.'

Problem solved I thought and took a triumphant swig of Bud.

'I've got a hammer in the trunk,' Andy said, 'I can go and get it.'

For the first time ever, JK, who is the reigning champion of Heath Robinson bicycle maintenance, was hesitant.

'I think I'll see how it goes tomorrow, it just seems a little too drastic for my liking,' he said. And noticing Andy's disappointed expression, who was clearly relishing the prospect of the hammer treatment, added 'I'll bear it in mind for a last option though.'

Andy seemed to accept this excuse and he allowed us to sample some of his barbecue and a few more Budweisers. We stayed in their convivial company for a while before opting for an early night.

***

I was ambivalent about the prospect of our morning ride. Monty had raved about Mount Fleecer, which was the monolith we were now at the foot of. Indeed the trail notes give it the accolade of being one of the most memorable places on the Great Divide. However, I've come to realise that such a tribute usually comes at a price, and in this instance it was six slow miles of climbing. The sun didn't abate, indeed it put in a special effort as it observed the spectacle of two pitiful ants zigzagging their way up the mountain.

Just like when the answer to a trivia question comes to you at two o'clock in morning, it suddenly dawned on me half way up the climb. The reason Monty had raved about Mount Fleecer was because he had been riding in the opposite direction, he would have come flying down our present climb at ten times our current speed. This obvious, retrospective realisation knocked the wind out of my sails rendering the following two hours of climbing as torturous. In addition JK had to endure the maddening process of having to tighten his cranks every five to ten minutes. The descent was steep, too steep to ride, so we walked our bikes down, zigzagging through the sage bushes. Not being able to ride wasn't really an issue for me because the views were spellbinding and it is was good to experience them from a foveal perspective, rather than the usual fleeting peripheral snapshots. As the grade lessened and became manageable we remounted and cruised for about ten miles until we reached the next small hamlet: Wise River.

By the time we pulled up outside the mercantile, JK's cranks had deteriorated to an extent that they were rendered pretty much useless. We probably could have made it back to Butte if we had tuned back earlier, but that option was now academic. It seemed we were now screwed – the next bike shop on route wasn't for another four hundred miles and there was no way Vick could last the journey. The good news was that the mercantile sold fresh donuts and hazelnut coffee.

Clutching the food and coffee like my life depended on them, I waited patiently in line to be served. I was fatigued and hungry and was getting increasingly irritable at having to wait while the old boy in front of me blathered on about some mundane shit or other. Through my sunglasses I fixed the back of his head with my glare and tried to use

55

the power of thought to make him leave. Or die. I wasn't too bothered which. I caught myself thinking this and said to myself, 'come on, be positive, the old guy is just talking, it will be your turn soon enough.' It was then that a little kid of around five years old stepped out from behind some shelves and smiled at me. In my newly found positive frame of mind I crouched down on my haunches so that I could be at his level. I moved my shades onto the top of my head so as not to scare him, and noticing that he was hiding something behind his back I asked, 'and what have you got there?'

The kid was obviously a descendant of a Wild West gunslinger because in one fluid movement he produced a neon plastic water pistol (actually it looked more like a Kalashnikov) he deftly pumped the primer and with sniper-accuracy he power-hosed my right eye. Startled and in pain I lost my balance and toppled backward. From my ungainly position I blinked hard, but could not focus on the small bleary figure that appeared to be pumping the primer once more. Then I felt a jet of water hit my crotch. The little kid disappeared into the isles giggling.

Under the gaze of the shop assistant and the old boy, I picked myself up and tried to muster as much dignity as I could despite having what looked like a piss stain down the front of my shorts.

'Don't mind him,' the shop assistant advised.

It was pretty difficult not to mind him, but being the diplomat that I am, I replied, 'oh, it's okay.' As I did so I felt a jet of water hit my arse. Little twat.

After my shopping debacle I basked on the porch outside the shop in an attempt to dry off and as the fat and caffeine oozed into my arteries, the hassle of our predicament melted away.

'I suppose our only option is to phone up the bike shop in Butte and get them to FedEx us a new crank to here,' I mumbled between bites of stodge and swigs of coffee, 'we'll just have to camp here until it arrives.'

Mellowed by his refection, JK philosophically agreed, and to show his endorsement he purchased another round of six donuts.

'HARDCORE!' came a booming voice from an old man getting out of his truck. He was apparently talking to us. He made his way over and extended his arm. 'Dick Dodge is the name.'

Dick was a tall, wiry cowboy with the appearance of Sam Elliott in The Big Lebowski, only without the moustache. He was a fit, sixty one year old, who was originally from Wise River, but these days he lives in South Dakota with his wife. He was here on vacation, living in his trailer and riding his motorcycle along the numerous trail networks and checking out the plethora of stunning lakes he visited in his youth (I was later to learn that he totalled seventy seven lakes during the summer). He was genuinely impressed by our trip and bombarded us with a never ending stream of questions. When we told him about the cranks, there was only one possible solution.

'We'll put them in the back of my truck and I'll give you a lift to Butte,' he offered, 'course I'll have to ask you for a couple of bucks for gas, I wouldn't ask but I'm retired now.'

'No problem,' came our synchronised reply.

It was about a fifty mile drive back to Butte and as we sped north along Interstate 91, Dick told us his life story and educated us with his encyclopaedic knowledge of the surrounding area. After twenty one years in the Air Force working on B1 Bombers, Dick embarked on a career of eating shit for, and getting shafted by, large corporations. Then after he retired he returned to doing what he loved most – riding his motorcycle in the wilderness around his birthplace. His dream would be to retire here, but his wife has put the kibosh on it and doesn't want to live in such a remote place. I could see both sides of the story.

What would have been a day's worth of cycling raced by in less than ninety air-cooled minutes, and before I knew it we were outside the bike shop in Butte. JK brought the sales assistant up to speed with the state of Vick; the assistant sucked on his teeth and said, 'I don't think we've got any cranks in stock, but I'll go and check with the mechanic.'

And with that he disappeared into the workshop.

'We should be alright,' I said to JK pointing at a couple of bikes hanging from the ceiling, 'those bikes have got the cranks you need, so if push comes to shove they can take a pair off one of those and replace it when the order comes in.'

The assistance reappeared, 'I'm sorry, but we haven't got any in stock.'

JK informed him about our trip and asked if we could have a set of cranks off one of the display bikes.

'I'm sorry those cranks come with the bikes and it is not shop policy to take bits off them,' he robotically responded.

'I appreciate that mate, but we're stuck in a hole. Can't you make an exception just this once?' JK pleaded.

'If it was my shop I would, honestly,' he reasoned, 'but the owner would kill me.'

Fair enough, I didn't want the guy to get the sack, well to be honest I wasn't really bothered, but I suppose he had a point. So off we dourly traipsed, back to Dick's truck.

I was feeling a little despondent, but Dick was pretty upbeat about the situation. He seemed to be relishing the idea of a challenge and that maybe he could be the hero and save the day.

'I know a little bike store over in Anaconda, we can go and check that out if you like?'

Of course we gratefully agreed.

Anaconda was a hell of a place. Indeed it ranks as the grimmest place I have ever been, and bearing in mind that I am a Northerner, that's one hell of a comment. It is a small mining village whose skyline is dominated by a pair of huge slagheaps. Dick informed me that the two carbuncles were heavy metal deposits resulting from one hundred years of gold mining. Apparently, the toxins are by-products of fractional distillation, a process whereby the earth is smelted and the metal ore is run off. The good stuff gets removed and used and the crap is left behind; the slagheaps are the toxic crap. Furthermore, mercury is used to enhance the extraction.

The slagheaps on their own were bad enough, but my lasting and haunting memory of the place was how everything downwind from them was barren, or if the odd tree did survive it was stunted. Surprisingly the poisonous effects of these dust mounds didn't appear to bother the residents, who seemed happy to go about their business with this sword of Damocles hanging above them. I may be doing it a grave disservice, but to me Anaconda is a dark shadow on the lung of Montana.

From the outside the bike shop did not look promising, it was just a regular house with a sign that read: Zven's Bicycles of Anaconda. Yet once inside I knew we were in good hands; Pete Kurtz, the proprietor was a laid-back cycle fanatic who calmly assessed the situation and was glad to lend a hand. He put Vick on his work stand and began to ply his trade. The problem, it transpired, wasn't JK's cranks after all. Instead his bottom bracket had been rounded off – which isn't as painful as it sounds. With a new bottom bracket fitted, Pete torqued the cranks back on with a surprisingly large wrench, he had obviously heard of the Chicago fit as well. Concerned, JK asked him if he should be applying so much force,

'Yeah, you wanna get about thirty five psi,' he grunted, 'which is when the veins in my forearms pop out. If the veins in my temples pop out then I've done forty – which is too much.'

His face was red, but thankfully there were no veins.

'There you go, that should get a couple of trailhounds like you back on the road,' Pete commented, stepping back to admire his craftsmanship.

Trailhound – that's a fair accolade especially coming from a hardened bicycle enthusiast like Pete. I wonder if this means that I am now a cyclist? Just in case I was, I thought I had better keep the esoteric conversation going,

'Pete I've got to ask, why have you called your shop Zven's?'

'Well, I used to work in a ski shop in Whitefish and the Norwegian skiers used to call me Zven.'

Of course, how silly of me.

On the way back to Wise River, Dick produced a round of the appropriately named Fat Tire Beer from his cooler. We toasted Pete and chewed the fat over a couple more as we headed back. Although our displacement was zero, we had experienced a phase shift of about six hours. Despite wanting to have a couple more beers with Dick, we had to push on, and so we reluctantly said our farewells. After a few more hours of riding it was getting late, so we checked in at a trailside motel called the Grasshopper Inn and enjoyed the rare luxuries of real food, showers and real beds.

***

The alarm went off far too early, and I found it really difficult to get out of bed. If there was ever a time I needed coffee this was it, but the ungodly hour meant that no one was serving it. There wasn't even any crappy make-it-yourself kit in the room. JK was up at first light and was the main driving force behind getting me back on the trail. It was a cold morning as we pedalled our way south along the open plains of southwest Montana. As the sun rose it became easy to see why this area is known as "Big Sky Country", it was the only thing to see for miles. Yesterday's dearth of miles meant that we had to take up the slack and put in a hard ride. Our unspoken aim was to put in a century ride and get to Lima, which according the map has a campground, accommodation, petrol, food and a post office. Which could mean that it has all mod cons, or indeed it could turn out to be a ghost town last inhabited by nineteenth century miners. Either way, getting to Lima would put us back in the ballpark of being able to complete the route on time.

The profile for the next hundred miles was, according to the map, generally in our favour; it was relatively flat, the only anomaly being a two thousand foot climb up to a place called Sheep Creek Divide. Fortunately the climb was distributed over thirty miles, which in theory would mean the gradient wasn't too severe. Our early start meant there was no hurry, as long as we kept turning the pedals we would eventually get there without any stress – a bit like an Amtrak train.

During the first part of the day we followed a section of the Lewis and Clark Historic Trail, which follows in the footsteps of their Corps of Discovery when they

59

explored the uncharted west. As such our morning ride was littered with historic anecdotes and stories. One such tale is about a Shoshone Indian called Sacagawea. Around1800 at the age of twelve, she was kidnapped by the Hidatsa Indians, the sworn enemy of her people and was taken to Hidatsa-Mandan and sold as a wife to a French-Canadian fur trader. A few years later the Corps of Discovery arrived at Hidatsa-Mandan and built a fort there. They intended to trade for horses with the Shoshone Indians so that they could continue their expedition, and to make the exchange easier they took Sacagawea along as a translator. By a remarkable twist of fate Sacagawea recognised the Indian Chief, Cameahwait as her long lost brother. Needless to say, the reunion helped Lewis and Clark with their horse trading.

After several hours of Amtraking, it became apparent that the map profiles weren't particularly accurate. On the map legend it reads: "This profile is intended to show you only the general elevation of the route, allowing you to plan for major climbs and descents." I think the word "general" is too precise, and should be replaced with something far more nebulous. It should read something like this: "This wiggly line is intended to show you *an* elevation of *a* route (not particularly this one), allowing you to plan for nothing."

However there was solace to be had. Even John Stamstad had been a little cheesed off with the imprecise cartography, in an article for Airbourne.net, he writes:
'...if the next 100 miles was made up of two mile climbs followed by two mile descents (no net gain) the map will show this as a flat line. There's a big difference between riding two mile rollers all day and riding the flats.'

And to make things a little more difficult even the rollers had rollers. The dirt roads had, as a result of motorised traffic I presume, an undulated appearance, which is like riding mile upon mile of frozen ripples, each with the amplitude and frequency of corrugated iron. Exactly how four-wheel drive vehicles give rise to them I am unsure (even after spending several hours a day thinking about it), but the little bastards had been exactly the same for the last few days. They render coasting obsolete, and take the fun out of descents, not to mention taking the piss out my woefully inadequate nappy cream defence. The only saving grace was that we had front suspension on our bikes. Whoops, I spoke too soon.

With a remarkable, mechanical fluidity that is usually only reserved for Swiss clocks, or German cars Vick somehow managed to synchronise losing his grip on JK's saddle whilst simultaneously blowing the oil seal on his suspension. This forced an unsuspecting JK to perform an impromptu Mexican wave/retro breakdance move for several unbecoming metres before being unceremoniously dumped on the trailside. Once again he kicked Vick. The saddle was easily resolved, it was just a loose bolt, but the suspension was well and truly knackered. With the oil seal blown, there was no dampening on the suspension unit, which meant that after each bump Vick repeatedly pogoed up and down, causing JK to feel seasick. It was a long nauseous day in the saddle for JK, for me it wasn't too bad because riding next to me I had a tangible benchmark of just how bad things could get. And for that I was grateful.

Many times we thought about a premature trailside camp, but that would not be doing ourselves any favours further down the line. We had a set distance to cover in a finite amount of time; cut ourselves slack now and we would have to make up the shortfall later. Faced with no feasible alternative we monotonously pedalled onward, eventually arriving in Lima. In our hour of need the map pulled through. With the exception of the campground, the map symbols next to Lima actually translated into real facilities, there was: a café, a gas station, a post office and accommodation. We patronised them in that order.

We discussed our options over a hamburger supper at Jan's Café and were in such a dilemma that our deliberations spilled over into a second, then a third helping of cherry pie. The only real option we had was to make a detour to the next available bike shop. There were three contenders: Dubois (two hundred and seventy miles away), Pinedale (three hundred and ten miles away), and Jackson (two hundred and nineteen miles away) – not just a pop down to the shops by anyone's standards. We quickly slipped into a routine; I ordered a round of cherry pies whilst JK phoned a bike shop, he'd come back and say that it didn't exist, or it was essentially a hardware store that had earned bike shop status because it had once sold an inner tube back in the Seventies. We would then eat the cherry pie and repeat the process. Fortunately (or unfortunately) because it heralded the end of the pies Jackson looked promising. After stocking up on Little Debbie snacks and other gas station culinary delights we checked in at the Lima Motel and drew a line under a hard day.

***

The fear of death is just as good a kick-start first thing in the morning as a caffeine boost. At the gas station counter I groggily asked the teenage attendant if he sold coffee (full hit this time, not decaf).

'Yeah, hang on I'll make you a fresh pot,' he replied and after taking my cash for the coffee and the dozen doughnuts I had procured, he casually made his way over to the coffee machine.

'Can you bring them out to us?' I asked, 'we'll just be on the forecourt with the bikes.'

'Sure, no problem. Hey, are you guys doing the Great Divide?'

'Yeah, how do you know about it?' I asked.

'We had an Aussie guy in here yesterday who was riding it, or was it the day before?' he replied, then added, 'you folks are crazy.'

'Thanks.' I said sarcastically.

'You're welcome,' he countered, perhaps sarcastically.

Outside we stood around Vick munching doughnuts and looking at his suspension unit. We had the general demeanour of council workers looking at a pending job. A short while later the gas station door opened and the attendant brought us our coffees. He then joined us looking at Vick. When he bent down to have a closer look, he casually removed the cigarette from his mouth and flicked the lit butt behind him. It arced through the air bounced off a petrol pump and fell to the floor.

'CHRIST!' JK shouted turning to shield himself from the impending blast.

'What's up?' said the attendant straightening himself up.

'You could have blown us all sky high,' I protested leaping and stamping on the butt.

'It's never caught fire before,' he said defensively, and as he headed back inside he defiantly sparked up another one.

JK and I glanced at each other, it was time to get back on the trail.

I was riding along looking down at my front wheel when I was woken from my cyclical mantra by what appeared to be fresh bike tracks. There were three distinct tyre treads, but the way they meandered and blended together meant that they all belonged to the same rider, a Great Divide soloist dragging a trailer, no doubt the Aussie. They must have been made today because it only takes a couple of four-wheel drive vehicles to blast down the trail and their dusty wake wipes the slate clean of any tracks. JK was riding a few hundred yards behind me, so I dropped my pace so that he could catch up and I could find out if he had noticed them. As he pedalled closer it became apparent that he was in a lot of pain. He was wincing with every down stroke of his left leg. He stopped when he reached me, laid Vick down and shook his head.

'I don't know what's happened, but it feels like part of my thigh muscle is torn,' he said in a resigned tone.

'What do you want to do?' I inquired.

'I don't know, I really don't,' he answered, looking pained.

Our first aid kit consisted of only antiseptic cream, nappy rash cream and Ibuprofen, Vitamin I it was to be then, and in extra large doses. We rested for a while and then set off again albeit at a slower pace. After about ten minutes I looked over my shoulder to see JK a few hundred yards back pushing Vick. Things must be bad, in all of the time I have known him I have never seen him pushing, it must have been eating him up inside. I dismounted and waited for him and then together we pushed our bikes up the gentle incline out of Lima. The silence was worrying.

We stopped at the top of the rise.

'I have an idea about what might have caused it,' I offered.

JK silently nodded for me to continue.

'Maybe it's the change in saddle position after it slipped yesterday.'

JK snorted in a derisorily manner and shook his head, 'I don't think so, but let's give it a try.'

He fettled around with his saddle for a while, perhaps more for my benefit than his own, and then we coasted down the other side of the hill. I let JK take the lead so that he didn't have to play catch up, and so that I could ride by myself and try and work out what we were going to do. My main concern was our food and water supplies. We had packed the bare minimum for the eighty-odd mile ride to Macks Inn, which was the nearest place to restock. It was about a day's ride away, but at this pace we were going to be lucky if we would make it halfway. I was pondering whether we should head back to Lima, when I noticed that JK was at the foot of the descent poised with his camera ready to take my picture. He must have been feeling better, because bothering with a camera is usually the last thing on your mind when the hassles start piling up.

'How is it?' I tentatively inquired, slowing down along side him.

'Still fucking sore,' he replied, 'but the Vitamin I has taken the edge off and I think the saddle has helped a bit. The whole geometry is screwed,' and pumping the dead suspension he added, 'so if we get to Jackson I reckon I'm gonna have to buy a new bike.'

Oh well things weren't so bad, there were a few positives in there somewhere. Slowly, and painfully for JK, we pedalled east along the primitive dirt roads, still following the other bike tracks. As we passed above Upper Red Rock campground we saw the machine responsible for them; a loaded mountain bike and trailer propped up next to a tent. One of the panniers sported the Australian flag. We shouted down but there was no response, he was either trying to get some sleep, or ignoring us and hoping we would go away. Either way, I can't really blame him.

I would like to think I am above ego trips, but apparently I'm not. Passing the Aussie while he was asleep somehow made me feel superior – a better cyclist almost.

Quite how I arrived at this notion I have absolutely no idea, but it seemed to have had the same effect on JK, to the extent that it put a little verve back into his knackered leg. 'Let's go,' he whispered, 'the more distance we can get on him the better.'

We entered the wetlands of Red Rock Lakes National Wildlife Reserve situated close to the Montana/Idaho border and took a well-earned rest at Lakeview, the Reserve's headquarters. The 42,525-acre Reserve was principally created to help protect the beautiful trumpeter swans' dwindling population, which was a result of hunting and the destruction of their habitat due to the draining of the wetlands. It seems the programme has been successful, because in the last seventy years the headcount of trumpeter swans has risen from under one hundred to a maximum of two thousand. Other animals also seek sanctuary here including moose, elk and bald eagles. I wondered if they would be able to do anything for a couple of weary trailhounds.

The rangers were very helpful and let us refill our water supplies, use their telephone and their computer. Our two hours spent there were surprisingly successful, we escaped the heat and completed some necessary admin work. With a flurry of phone calls and emails we managed to locate a spare part for JK's suspension unit at The Edge Cyclery in Jackson. Buoyed by not having to purchase a complete bike and no doubt by the vast quantities of Vitamin I he was consuming, he seemed in better spirits. We headed off for Red Rock Pass, which has the dual status of being Continental Divide crossing number six and also the border of Idaho.

JK pulled up at the state border sign and wanted his picture taken next to it. He posed, I took the shot, and then he muttered,
'I'll be glad to see the back of Montana.'
He was in good company. When John Stamstad finished the route he was interviewed for Mountainzone.com and asked if he was glad it was over. Stamstad mused, 'I was ready for it to be over in Montana.'
A few miles down the trail we pulled into an RV Park. We were completely knackered and in need of a hot shower. The site manager was affable and very helpful, but I couldn't help being appalled by his laziness – he had taken sloth to a new level. He was sitting on a porch bench outside the reception when we approached him and inquired about pitching our tent. The park was busy but he reassured us that he would find us a site. He stood up, stepped off the porch and threw his leg over his all wheel drive (AWD) quad bike, fired it up and ambled off at about walking pace. I assumed that our pitch was going to be over the other side of the park. JK and I started pushing our bikes along side him and just as I started to engage Mr Sloth in a conversation he killed his engine.

'Here you go,' he said, pointing at a flat patch of earth, 'just be careful to watch those water pipes when you're sticking your tent pegs in the ground.'

We had literally walked twenty paces and he had needed his AWD. After a brief chat he fired it back up again and trundled back to the porch to resume eating ice cream. Maximum pleasure, minimum effort. For some reason I was feeling very moralistic, perhaps it was because, for once, I wasn't using the earth's limited resources unnecessarily. Or perhaps my self-importance stemmed from being self-sufficient, human powered and at one with nature. Or maybe, just maybe, I was as jealous as hell that his bike had an internal combustion engine and mine didn't.

CHAPTER SIX. RED ROCK TO ATLANIC CITY

'always concede to local knowledge'

After a brisk early morning ride we were more than ready for breakfast when we joined civilisation at Interstate 20. During our travels little truisms have developed, the most prominent one being: if there is an Interstate there is a gas station and if there is a gas station there is junk food. JK went straight for the coffee machine, whilst I paced the isles in search of doughnuts and trail fodder. We placed all of our items on the counter – which amounted to two rucksacks worth. Normally I'd be ashamed of consuming such crap food, but I was so hungry I was tucking into it whilst I was queuing.

'You guys doin' the bike ride thing?' asked the middle aged attendant, whose flaccid physique indicated he wasn't averse to putting away a bit of the old junk food either. He added, 'we've had a few riders through this last month.'

'Yeah, we're doing the Divide,' JK replied, and inquired as to whether Rosy and Stuart had passed through. The attendant wasn't sure, he hadn't served them but someone else might have. He handed us our confectionary in two large brown paper bags.

'You need the energy, right?' he said in a tone that indicated this was the same lie he told himself every time he indulged in candy, and then added, 'you guys must be fit.'

He then did something that startled all three of us – he struck a short series of unbecoming muscle poses. Unfortunately none of his muscles tensed, or if they did they weren't visible under his rotund subcutaneous layer, and as such he rendered the little routine as nothing more than a cannon shuffle. We all silently looked at each other. Then he broke the awkwardness with a Muttley-esq chortle, to which JK and I obligingly chipped in.

'You guys take care,' he said, signalling the end of his ignominy.

'Thanks, and you,' I replied.

'You're welcome.'

Outside I munched my doughnuts and sipped my coffee whilst basking in the sun. The previous week I would have taken shelter under the shade of the gas station canopy, so I assumed that my body must have adapted to the heat. We topped up our water from a standpipe awkwardly poking out of the concrete forecourt and set off in the direction of a dirt track that would lead us to an old Union Pacific spur line that ran between Yellowstone and a place called Ashton.

'Hey, you're going the wrong way,' our attendant friend hollered from the doorway, 'most folk take the road from here,' he said pointing in the opposite direction.

'Okay, thanks,' I said.

'You're welcome,' he replied returning inside.

'That's not what it says here,' JK commented pointing to the map.

He was right, it was definitely straight ahead along the dirt road. We ignored the attendant's advice and followed the map. Within the next ten minutes I learned an important lesson: always concede to local knowledge. The reason why the previous riders had chosen the blacktop was because it was the slicker hypotenuse of a triangle whose other sides comprised several inches of potash, routinely interrupted with depressions left by old railway sleepers. It was like cycling in rippled sand, and we were forced to hack out of the saddle for about an hour only to return to the road, which would have been an easy half-hour cruise. Yielding to Nietzsche's philosophy, the volcanic ash gave way to a beautiful ride through wetlands with several water crossings, and what's more it was ever so slightly downhill.

We coasted down into a valley which had been fashioned by the merging of two rivers, Warm River and the North Fork of the Snake River. If time had permitted I would have liked to have established whether Warm River lived up to its name, but I was content to take the latter at face value. This confluence is a geographical boundary delineating the canyon country we've been cycling through and the wide open fields that lay before us. We cycled into our new surroundings and headed up a gentle incline towards the Idaho-Wyoming border, situated at around six and a half thousand feet above sea level. Although we only cut the corner of Idaho I was chuffed to be entering our third state, and seeing as we only have to cover five states in total, I somehow managed to convince myself that we were three fifths of the way there.

The trail became fairly rugged when we entered Teton County and we pulled up at a juncture that just begged us to camp there. JK was drawn to the primitive campground perched on the water's edge of the picturesque Grassy Lake Reservoir. But I was more influenced by the formidable rocky ascent that loomed ahead; I figured that could wait until tomorrow. Despite JK and Vick being the worse for wear, we had still managed a respectable eighty miles which just kept the carrot, that we might actually finish the ride, on the horizon. We silently slipped into the routine of setting up camp, with each of us knowing exactly what our tasks were. JK set about fixing our meal (Chinese flavoured noodles) and I went down to the water's edge and systematically broke our water filter.

Noodles are pretty difficult to eat out of a shared cookpot and by the time we had finished my face was covered in pseudo Chinese sauce.

'Chuck me a baby wipe will you?' I asked JK, as he got up to retrieve his diary from his bar bag. He threw me the packet and commented,

'I think it is the last one.'

There was actually two left and I removed one to wipe my face. But I paused and thought about my action.

'I suppose I had better save them for our arses,' I mumbled, returning it to the packet.

'Christ, it's a hell of a situation when your arse comes before you face,' JK laughed, wiping sauce of his chin and licking his fingers.

'Well it is a good job I saved you one, or you might be having to do same with your backside,' I commented, nodding at his face cleaning gesture.

***

The familiar "beep", "beep" of JK's Suunto watch (which had somehow been given the nickname: Eddy the Army watch) came around far too early. I blinked at the blue nylon ceiling then realised where I was. "Beep", "beep" Eddy persisted.

I shuffled around the camp like the condemned man that I was, as soon as breakfast and packing were over I was about to experience the pain of an early morning technical climb. They were the worst - straight out of bed and into the thick of it. My lagging cardiovascular system did its utmost to match the demands of the climb, but it took all of my resolve to keep the cranks turning. It was only when I got my second wind that I realised we were brushing alongside Yellowstone National Park and I was able to marvel at its beauty. It was the pictures of landscape photographer William Henry Jackson that initially influenced Congress to establish Yellowstone as the world's first national park. This idea of designating areas as national parks has become a land-use template the world over. And since its modest beginnings, Yellowstone has been promoted to a Biosphere Reserve and then to a World Heritage Site. We continued skirting the beautiful park for a few miles then followed Snake River for a short while, before turning off onto Highway 287/191.

Highway 287/191 forms part of the grandiose Transamerica Bicycle Trail, which was, as far as I could determine, just a long stretch of blacktop. That said, not many roads are flanked with lakes as beautiful as Jackson Lake, whilst simultaneously being bordered by a majestic mountain range like the Tetons. The Tetons, which jut out of the ground like giant molars, acquired their peculiar name back in the early 1800s when homesick French-Irquois trappers ventured into the valley and stumbled upon the

68

awesome sight. Perhaps due to their celibacy, the trappers called the mountains les Trios Tetons – the Three Breasts. They do indeed look remarkably like a certain part of the female anatomy, so much so that later, British trappers called them 'The Three Paps', and oh how I wish that name had stuck. Of course we had our own adolescent names for them – but I would rather not go into that now.

We followed the Transamerica Bicycle Trail for twenty five miles to Moran Junction, the intersection of Highway 287/191 and Highway 26/89. Yet, it was more than just a highway crossroads – our fate lay in the decision we had to make there. We could continue east for fifty five miles on Highway 287/191 to the bike shop at Dubois in the hope that it had the suspension part for Vick, or turn south for thirty miles on Highway 26/89 to the cyclery in Jackson. We chose the latter.

If you think of a rectangle, the Great Divide route travels east from Moran Junction along Transamerica Bicycle Trail (Highway 287/191), then heads south, mostly on roads, to Pinedale. Our revised diversion, first heads south to Jackson, then traverses east to Pinedale. It is as broad as it is long, only our tarmac isn't called the Transamerica Bicycle Trail. Bummer! The asphalt proved to be a timely respite for JK who was getting increasingly beaten up because of his non-existent suspension. I took point duty for this stretch of the journey, thus giving him the opportunity to draft in my slipstream and take the pressure off his injured leg. After about twenty five miles of enduring an incessant headwind we entered Moose, a small village that surprisingly had a bike shop. I say surprisingly, because there is no mention of it on the map, but then again I suppose that isn't really a surprise. The shop was a cool set up. It was an open fronted shack fitted out with all of the latest doodads and had the Tetons as a magnificent backdrop. It looked like it would be a great place to work. The laid back assistant tried his best to help us with Vick's suspension woes, but his rummaging around in the loft proved fruitless. We talked for a while about the merits of various suspension systems and after looking at my suspension forks (Marzocchi Atom Race) he commented,

'How are the Marzocchis, have they held up?'

'Yeah, I've had no trouble at all,' I replied, and then rather perturbed I asked, 'why, don't you reckon they're up to the job?'

He screwed up his face, shrugged his shoulders and tutted a few times before philosophically mumbling, 'I'm sure they'll be okay.'

Well, thanks for the vote of confidence. Up until then I hadn't given them a second thought, they had performed faultlessly. I walked over to Corsair pressed down on the handlebars and pumped the suspension unit a few times. I convinced myself there was a bit of stiction and then consciously reeled in the negative thought; no it was just a nocebo effect, the proof was in the pudding and they've put in a sterling performance so far. However, he had sewn the seed of doubt, so in order to allay my paranoia I squirted some oil at them. Sorted.

Once again, I pointed the figurehead into the relentless wind, and this time lead us into Jackson. When we finally arrived I was physically washed up and judging by the grimace on JK's face his muscle injury was giving Vitamin I a serious run for its money. Despite the fatigue, we had to override our desire to find accommodation and we pressed on with the sleep deprivation torture for a little longer – top of our agenda was getting Vick repaired. The Edge Cyclery was easy to locate but I doubted that the spare part would be. Vick is a six year old Cannondale with a unique suspension system located within the frame. These suspension units have evolved considerably since then and I'd be surprised if that particular model is still manufactured. JK had already come to terms with purchasing a new bike, but asked about the spare part nonetheless. The mechanic looked at Vick, who was in a particularly poor state of repair, stroked his goatee and headed off into the workshop. He reappeared clutching the replacement part.

'You guys are real lucky,' he said, 'this is the only one we've got, it's been kicking around in the workshop for years, I'm surprised it hasn't been thrown out.'

The worthless spare part that he held in his grasp had morphed in a potential golden goose that was capable of laying a considerable golden egg. Providing it was less than the cost of a new bike, JK would pay the asking price. Vick was given a stay of execution and taken into the workshop, whilst JK paced up and down like an expectant father wondering what the outcome would be.

'Good as new,' was mechanic's prognosis as he wheeled Vick out from the workshop. JK immediately pounced on Vick and vigorously pumped the suspension unit. 'It's fixed!' he beamed.

And then a wave of reality kicked in, no doubt induced by my over-the-barrel experience in Helena. And with an ashen faced he asked the mechanic how much it was going to cost.

'Let's call it twenty six dollars,' the mechanic said punching the price into the till.

Twenty six dollars, what a bargain! For fear of crying, I made a conscious effort not to ask him how much a new set of cranks were. JK then blew a large chunk of the money he had saved on a celebratory meal.

Jackson is an affluent town and as such the majority of its hotels and motels were priced out of our modest – no, pitiable – budget. Just when I resigned myself to a night under canvas on the outskirts of town, we stumbled across the Anvil Motel Hostel. A young, bohemian looking Art Garfunkel was tending reception and he kindly gave us a quick tour. It was a cheap and cheerful affair, bunk beds were arranged in a dormitory style, there was a social TV lounge, and there was also a storeroom for Vick and Corsair. We spent the evening planning our route for the next few days. Coming up soon was a two to three day desert crossing and with it the problems of carrying water. So far, the summer had been uncharacteristically hot and as such even reliable water sources were drying up. Before tackling the desert we really needed to know what the water status was, but no one in Jackson had any information. Our only option was to wait until we got to Pinedale and check with the Rangers there.

JK suggested that we should have a day's rest and recharge our batteries before tackling the difficult days ahead. Of course I denounced the idea and insinuated that he was a wuss. And on that particular moral high note I indignantly retired to bed. The next morning I didn't hear Eddy's shrill calls to get me out of my bunk, instead JK had to wake me. I looked at him groggily, mentioned something about letting him have a rest day, and then fell fast asleep for twelve hours straight.

That evening I actually managed to have a normal telephone conversation with Wendy, but she annoyingly kept referring to the Great Divide as a holiday. I went to great lengths to explain to her how gruelling it all was, and then after our conversation I retired to the couch and watched television all night. Whilst flicking through the channels I stumbled across some live coverage of The Tour de France, and was haunted by an image of Lance Armstrong beating his opponents into submission on a particularly gruelling climb. The juxtaposition was intense, on the screen there was a real cyclist, whilst on the couch there was a pretender. I rectified the situation with a deft press of the remote control.

***

During my comatose state the previous day, JK had the presence of mind to suss out a gas station that would be open during the early hours, and it was here that we started Day Fourteen with our usual stodge and decaf. We knew from the outset that the ride to Pinedale was going to be a boring one. It was a seventy-odd mile road ride, the monotony of which was only broken every hour with a Fig Newton break. Mountain biking off-road is an intense experience as it requires a lot of concentration, whereas cruising along on the road for a day allows one's brain to be idle. This of course is a dangerous situation. If I wasn't killing time talking crap with JK, my subconscious mind would throw up all kinds of weird stuff from the vaults deep within my head. Worryingly most of the stuff was retro Eighties songs, which I was surprised to find I knew the lyrics to (this is especially strange because I didn't know the proper lyrics when they were in the charts). Then again my weirdness paled into insignificance compared to the strange stuff JK was singing.

We arrived in Pinedale at mid-afternoon. It's a real cowboy town with guys walking around wearing dusty wranglers and jangling spurs. In between wads of tobacco being spat, I managed to decipher the directions to a campsite, and also learned that an English couple who were riding the Great Divide were also in town, they must be Rosie and Stuart. We pulled onto the campsite and JK went into reception to sort out the admin, whilst I remained outside with the bikes. I noticed a guy with a rucksack propping himself up against the ramshackle building that was the reception. I nodded a 'hello' at him, but he didn't respond even though he was looking me in the eyes. Feeling uneasy, I busied myself with something on Corsair.

'Hi,' came the overdue response.

'Hi,' I replied, and in attempt to engage in conversation I added, 'where are you heading?'

Again, no reply. There was something odd about this guy, he was about my age but his posture was crooked and he had a weird stare. He looked like he had just come back from a horrific war. I again busied myself with some superfluous task and mentally prompted JK to hurry up.

'I'm walking the Continental Divide, heading to Canada,' he answered.

Earlier on in the ride I had read an inscription in a café guest book written by a Continental Divide walker, it read: 'In my search for the illusive water, I have sung all of the songs and thought all of my thoughts…' and I remember thinking how hard it must be to walk alone for five or six months. Now I had the hard evidence propped up in front of me and it didn't look pretty. I quizzed him about the availability of water in the desert and he just shook his head in a manner that suggested I shouldn't ask him that question because it was still a raw wound.

We pitched the tent next to one with a couple of bike trailers outside which we presumed belonged to Rosie and Stuart and then cycled into town to find the Ranger's station. The desert stretch of the route is known as the Great Divide Basin and in this particular area water doesn't run to the Pacific or the Atlantic, instead it leaches into the arid earth.

There is however a reservoir called the A and M reservoir in the desert, but whether there is water in it nobody was sure. The ranger didn't have any up-to-date information but she phoned through to someone she knew who had been up there recently. She relayed the conversation to us, 'he says the reservoir is as dry as a bone and what surface water there is stinks. Sorry guys, your best bet is to detour on State Highway 789, which skirts around the desert.'

We thanked her for her advice but it wasn't what we wanted to hear. I really wanted to ride across the desert, it was the only way I could exorcise the demon of the pseudo-cyclist on the couch who was content to watch real cyclists ply their trade. But, more to the point the detour was a lot further to ride.

Back at the campsite we finally met Rosie and Stuart. They were an amiable couple who were taking about fourteen weeks to complete the Great Divide including a bit of sightseeing along the way. They were amazed by how light we were travelling; we marvelled at the amount and succulent diversity of food they carried. We scrounged what we could, but there is a fine line between accepting what is offered and proactively going through their food cache. We may have overstepped the mark, I'm not sure.

JK and I each purchased an extra Camalbak drinking bladder just in case we decided to cross the Basin. We could now carry about sixteen litres of water between us, which was about one day's worth. A rough plan was hatching: if we travelled fast enough, and managed to locate some water on route we should make the crossing in about two days. This shouldn't be too bad, we might come out the other side a little thirsty but that could easily be slaked once we were out of the desert. As with all major decisions, we decided to eat and to sleep on it. Well JK did, I had a fitful night's sleep because JK was snoring. I don't suppose it was too loud, but within the confines of our miniscule tent the snuffling was magnified. But what was more irritating was I became aware of it and listened out for even the faintest noise.

Day fifteen started like all of the others before it, I woke up to Eddy's racket, wondered where the hell I was, before a dispirited reality wave washed over me, it signalled the start of a fourteen hour cycling shift. It is the same kind of feeling you get when lying in bed on a Sunday morning and then suddenly realise it is actually Monday. The worst part of each morning was slapping on the cold, clammy nappy cream and then easing my Lycra cycling shorts on over the top. There were a few minutes of slimy discomfort until the cream warmed up to my body temperature and then it became bearable.

73

We had decided to make a 5.00 am start because we needed to cover a lot of ground. The maps and trail notes showed there weren't any provisions until a place called Rawlins, two hundred and twenty five miles, or about two to three days away. It was always difficult in situations like these to decide what to do. Do we take three days' worth of food, or just two? If we decide on the former we have to carry extra weight, which will slow us down and definitely turn it into a three day slog. Whereas the latter decision means we will travel lighter and swifter, but if things take longer than anticipated we could easily find ourselves up shit creek (I actually scoured the map to see if shit creek existed, there are some weird named creeks in these parts). Three things persuaded me to go light. First I don't like going heavy, secondly I would be pissed off if I carried three days' worth of food and completed the distance in two, and thirdly JK persuaded me for the same two reasons.

We planned on cycling for a couple of hours to a small village called Boulder. We could have breakfast and stock up our trail snacks at the gas station there and then press on for twelve hours. Everything went to plan up until the gas station, which didn't open until eight o'clock. So we were forced to sit on the forecourt for an hour in pitiless silence, each of us thinking about the extra hour of sleep we could have had. As the proprietor unlocked the door she was almost knocked from her feet as we bowled into the store. With all the precision of an S.A.S. raid we maximised calorie and caffeine acquisition in minimum time.

JK set a personal best record that day. No, it wasn't the furthest he had ever cycled in one day, or anything physical like that. Rather it was gastronomic achievement that occurred on the gas station forecourt; he managed to eat six full sized Danish pastries for breakfast, whilst I only managed a disappointing four. Clearly relishing his display of superiority, JK assumed the role of alpha male and what's more he knew I knew it. In the land of the long-distance bikepacker, the one with the garbage gut reigns supreme. I was therefore ecstatic when he later puked up at our third Fig Newton stop. My ascendancy was seamless.

As the day wore on, the temperature seemed to increase exponentially. It was our first few tentative pedal strokes in desert country and it put paid to our gung-ho approach to crossing the Basin. We really needed to give it some serious thought, it would be very easy to die out here in this heat. Indeed the heat was already doing some strange things to me – I had a phenomenal craving for Gatorade, even though I had never had it before. The thought of guzzling on that strange coloured cold beverage was driving me insane. There aren't many foodstuffs that are blue, indeed eating or drinking

74

something that is blue goes against my instincts (probably a throwback from my student days when I consumed a lot of nauseous, blue bread), but I had developed a need, or addiction, if that is possible with a novel substance – for blue Gatorade.

Despite crossing the Continental Divide (our ninth crossing), the terrain wasn't too bad, we stayed at around seven thousand feet all day with only the odd thousand footer to climb. Towards the end of the day's ride we rode through a gap in the Rockies where South Pass City is situated. South Pass City is a small town with a big history; overland travellers have used it since the nineteenth century. Indians, mountain men, Oregon and Mormon Trail emigrants, Pony Express riders and gold prospectors have all used this corridor at some time or another. Paradoxically the early gold prospectors who travelled this route were unaware of the abundance of gold in the South Pass City hills.

South Pass City also lays claim to being the first state or territory giving women the right to vote, and also having the first female judge in America. But my lasting memory of the place was the brutally steep climb out past the now derelict Carissa gold mine. Indeed glancing across at the mine was the last thing I remember of the scenery, I then placed my head on my bar bag and tortuously ground my way upwards. I hadn't felt this bad since we were in Montana. Fortunately, Atlantic City was visible from the summit and according to the map there was beer, food and beds there. Separating us from these delights was a five mile descent, a perfect way to finish a long day in the saddle.

Think of a Spaghetti Western. Think of the quintessential bar scene, a silhouetted cowboy arrogantly walking through the saloon doors, slowly pacing up to the bar and ordering a Bourbon. Now picture a knackered waif, dressed in Lycra, pushing the bar door (even though it is clearly marked PULL), stumbling into the saloon and demanding a blue Gatorade. Not very becoming. Well, that was my introduction to the Atlantic City cowboy fraternity. However, they must have been used to oddballs dropping in unannounced because no one broke stride despite our uncomfortable entrance. On the contrary the barflies, who consisted of cowboys, gold prospectors and a truck driver were very hospitable, and we talked about trails, local history and our collective adventures for hours. We had our evening meal at the bar and as luck would have it, the proprietor had a cabin out the back, which he let us have the run of for only $55. It was a timely stay in comfortable surroundings. We were beginning to smell a bit and it gave us a chance to clean ourselves as well as do some laundry. A real bed was also a bonus. So, knackered, well fed and with a slight beer buzz I immediately fell into a deep sleep.

CHAPTER SEVEN. ATLANTIC CITY TO STEAMBOAT SPRINGS.

'think all of your thoughts and sing all of your songs'

What was a pleasing sight one day, Atlantic City in a valley, became objectionable the next. The free euphoric miles into the city now had to be clawed back, inch by agonising inch. Rain clouds hung in the air alongside the knowledge that today was the day we were to enter the Basin. At some indiscernible point, the decision to cross the desert had been silently made. Fortunately, the relatively cool weather was in our favour, but unfortunately the distant thunder was accompanied by a muted rumbling in my guts. It is pretty amazing (read: horrific) what two weeks of Fig Newtons can do to a man's gastro intestinal tract. It was so bad that I had to forgo our first two snack stops. I just stood and watched incredulously as JK devoured Snickers after Snickers. He looked smug, he knew that the mantle of alpha male had switched hands once again.

As desolate and isolated as the landscape was many people have travelled along this section of the route. It was here where the Oregon-Mormon, and Pony Express trails converged and it has been estimated that over three hundred and fifty thousand travellers used this passage between 1840 and 1860 alone. Many pioneers heading for the promised lands of Utah and Oregon died here either as a result of thirst or the harsh cold winters. Indeed the eerie Oregon-Mormon trail has been described as the 'longest graveyard in America'. A particularly horrific tragedy occurred in the 1850s when nearly seventy Mormons hauling their belongings in handcarts were caught out in this unforgiving landscape late one October when a merciless snowstorm claimed all of their souls. The tale certainly put our efforts and grousing into perspective.

Every now and again I would get painful neurological feedback from my abdomen and I could never quite work out whether it wanted feeding, or if the pressure build-up was about to be involuntarily released. Not wanting to find out I clenched my buttocks and consumed vast quantities of vitamin I. Although it is a phenomenal panacea, consuming Ibuprofen on an empty stomach is not recommended, nor for that matter is cycling with a clenched arse. Due to my forced abstinence during the snack breaks, I was running on empty and had to drastically reduce my pace, which was disconcerting because we still had the majority of the Basin left to ride. JK pushed on ahead, leaving me to doggedly follow in his tyre tracks. Occasionally I would catch the odd glimpse of other mountain bike tyre tracks etched into the barren ground. Judging by the different tread patterns it looked like four separate bikes had made them. Rosie and Stuart had told us that there were a group of Americans that were about a day's ride ahead of us - these tracks must belong to them. I felt a little reassured that other riders had chosen to ride the Basin. I don't know why this comforted me, they could easily have been as clueless as JK and myself.

JK was waiting for me at the crest of our tenth Continental Divide crossing. When I reached him the view was exactly the same as from the top of the previous one: a desolate landscape with a long windy trail snaking off into the distance.

'Snack break?' JK inquired.

'I can't eat mate, my guts are all screwed up,' I replied pathetically.

Although I'm sure JK was concerned about my wellbeing, he couldn't hide the look in his eyes as the ramifications of my abstinence registered; double helpings for him.

'You've gotta eat something John,' he advised between bites of Payday, then scanning the landscape he added, 'otherwise you'll bonk, and this is the last place you need a hypo.'

I shook my head dismally, 'the thought of eating makes me feel sick.'

'How about a Fig Newton?' he asked, rummaging around in his bag and then producing said item.

I retched.

'Or some crackers, they're reasonably plain.'

He threw me the crackers and I painstakingly nibbled my way through one of them. I washed it down with some water and managed to restrain a few further retches.

'I think we're gaining on them,' JK commented pointing at the tyre tracks, 'I reckon we'll be able to catch them before the end of the day.'

Through a hypoglycaemic haze I nodded as enthusiastically as possible and I couldn't help but notice how energetic JK was looking.

'How's your leg?' I asked.

'Not bad the Vitamin I seems to have done the trick.'

That was not what I wanted to hear, I know it sounds dreadful, but I really could have done with something to handicap JK. But before I could formulate any plans to do so, he had clipped into his pedals and was coasting into the monotonous and austere landscape.

The humble cracker seemed to have helped a little bit and so I adopted the philosophy of eating little and often. I stashed a packet of crackers in the external pocket of my bar bag and nibbled them while I was riding. My pace was pedestrian and I knew that I must have been infuriating JK, who was just as anxious to get across the desert as I was. Unfortunately it was the best I could do.

'JK!' I shouted at the top of my voice.

The distant figure stopped cycling and turned around to look in my direction, no doubt wondering what else was up his frail albatross.

I eventually pulled level and between gasps commented, 'we've just clocked up a thousand miles.'

JK's face lit up, probably because I didn't have any further impediments as apposed to the milestone distance. And noticing the fatigue and strain in my eyes, he diplomatically added, 'Cool that calls for a much needed break.'

We leant the bikes on their sides and sat down on the dry earth. JK devoured yet more chocolate whilst I just sucked my crackers with an abnormal amount of trepidation.

'How are the guts?' JK inquired.

'Not bad, they seem to be...' I trailed off, as I focused internally on an involuntary movement that was occurring in my bowels. I leapt up and ran a few meters, then downed my shorts and let nature take its course. One of the main problems with deserts is there is nothing to hide behind so I had to perform my duty fully exposed. Fortunately JK was repulsed by the ordeal and hid his face in his hands as well as looking in the opposite direction. At times like these you can't be too careful. The good news was that I felt rejuvenated and could stomach a little more food, the bad news was that after my little display my chances of regaining alpha male status had gone down the pan, quite literally.

My pace increased in line with my rising sense of wellbeing and even the gods seemed to have taken pity and gave us a helping hand; an evening tailwind was gently pressing on our backs. As we approached the A and M reservoir, I noticed three distant figures heading out of the desert. The caravan was moving fast enough to be cyclists so I assumed that they must have been the American group, but where was the missing fourth member? My concern for the lost cyclist was short lived, as we were presented with our own conundrum when we arrived at the reservoir. With hindsight reservoir is actually the wrong word for it. Crater is better. Apparently in 1999, as a result of a merger between BP and Amaco oil, water is no longer pumped into the reservoir. Why oil companies would be wanting to pump water instead of drilling for oil I don't know, but the Bureau of Land Management, who are responsible for the area, were apparently looking for alternative pumping methods. Of course, that information was of no help to us. Fortunately the relatively cool day, slower pace, and the favourable zephyr meant that our water consumption was lower than usual. We each had about three litres left, which should in theory be enough to see us out of the desert, so we decided to camp next to the crater.

Camping in the desert was a humbling experience, one of those new age kind of hippy experiences. All we needed was some piped in whale music and a few joss sticks and we were there. Motivated by the possibility that I was having a belated spiritual awakening before retiring for the night, I stood outside of the tent and looked out to the horizon. There was a blanket of eerie quietness so silent that I could here buzzing in my ears and about fifty meters in front of me, staring back, was a seagull. I was pondering the enormity of it all and how the seagull had come to be where he was, when I heard the ominous howl of a coyote. Thinking bollocks to this awakening, I dived into my sleeping bag and hid there until morning.

The following day, as you would expect, the scenery hadn't changed. It was another forty five miles of the same old same old. I had spent the last three days in these surroundings and it was starting to become somewhat monotonous; so much for my spiritual awakening. For those individuals who walk it, they would see the same thing for about two or three weeks. It is easy to imagine how you could think all of your thoughts and sing all of your songs if you were in that situation.

And just when the day's stimulation was at its lowest, a bit of trail gossip presented itself. I rode passed an "E" drawn in the dry earth, then a "C", followed by an "N", an "I" a "V" and finally an arrow pointing to a letter pierced with a stick. Naturally we didn't think twice about reading the note. On the outside of the folded paper was the name VINCE; ah, that makes more sense, I thought Ecniv was a strange name. The gist of the note was the authors explaining to Vince that they hoped he was okay and that they would be booked into the Days Inn in Rawlings if he wanted to rejoin them. JK replaced the note, and buoyed by a bit of tittle-tattle we cycled side by side and discussed the possible scenarios that could have lead to the note. Of course it was conjecture at best, and complete fabrication at worst. With only one hard fact, Vince's name, and a bit of filling in, the story goes like this: Vince was obviously the fourth person, who had been separated, or dumped, by the other three cyclists we had seen hot-tailing it out of the desert, presumably to the comfort of the Days Inn. Despite exploring all permutations, we couldn't work out where Vince could be; if he had fallen off the back of the group we surely would have passed him. That was the précis so far, I know it's not much, but it had taken us two hours of riding just to come up with that.

Our derisory speculation was happily interrupted by a couple of Continental Divide walkers. Stopping next to them, we all engaged in an intense conversation that only people who haven't seen anyone for days can. David and Mary were middle-aged mountain bike fanatics from Idaho who were green with envy that we were riding the route. I asked why they weren't riding it and they said that they wished they were, but years ago before the birth of mountain biking, they had planned to walk it and so they had no other option but to live out their first dream despite their more favoured alternative. They're a weird bunch these long distance walkers.

'How do you deal with the monotony of it all?' I asked.

'How do I deal with him more like,' Mary piped in nodding at David.

'Let me tell you, I've been married to this woman for over thirty years and I thought I really knew her. I didn't know the half of it until we started doing this walk,' David countered.

Uh oh, it was time to leave, we offered them some water, and wished them well.

Every so often the monotonous trailside was punctuated with huge, neat piles of manure, and I am talking huge – it's as though a dozen or so horses defecated in the same place. I let a few piles go past before quizzing JK for his view on how, or why they were there. It transpired that he was as clueless as me. One thing was for sure, a single horse could not be responsible for one pile. So who, or what, was?

Upon leaving the Basin and rejoining the Transamerica Bicycle Trail, Rawlings was the first urban area we encountered. It is a State Penitentiary town and to be honest I thought it was dump. There has been a penitentiary there for over a century, and the earliest one; the Old Frontier Prison housed Wyoming desperados and lawbreakers of the era, including the likes of Martha Jane Canary, who is more popularly known as Calamity Jane. Apparently she was incarcerated for a month in The Old Frontier prison for being drunk and disorderly. Her CV also includes the roles of laundress, stagecoach driver and prostitute. As a result of her lifestyle the community frowned upon her, but her friend Dora Dufran was quick to defend Calamity's actions by writing that she was not immoral, she was unmoral. I must remember that one the next time I prostitute myself on a stagecoach whilst drunkenly doing someone's laundry.

Rawlings sported a full service star on our map which thankfully translated into real services. We stopped at the first café we saw which was a glass fronted affair, and made ourselves familiar with the menu. First up was a coffee and a soup of the day, which gave me the sustenance to peruse the menu for the serious courses.

'Looks like some wacko has got his eye on our bikes,' JK said, returning from the public phone.

I looked across at the bikes which were leaning against the window, and sure enough there was a tramp-looking guy with a strange demeanour scrutinising our bikes. Just as I was about to go outside and challenge him, he came into the café and made a beeline for our table.

'Are yee doin' the Divide?' he said in a thick Scottish drawl. Or at least that is what I thought he said, 'do you mind if I sit doon? Me name's Robbie.'

Robbie was a serious bikepacker who was riding the trail as far as Denver with Julie a fellow Scot, who also pulled up a chair. We swapped trail stories and it wasn't long before the Vince scandal cropped up. Robbie and Julie had spent a few days on the trail with the American group and gave us a few more pieces for our jigsaw. Apparently Vince *et al.* had met via the Internet earlier on in the year. Remarkably the group hadn't met until the day they set off on the ride and they soon realised that the group dynamics weren't ideal. It became clear early on that the group comprised riders of different abilities, the giveaway being that one member was being towed up the first climb out of Eureka with a bungee. But it doesn't stop there; another rider – the strongest – was six months pregnant. Despite their incongruous abilities and personalities the group felt bound, for some inexplicable reason as they were all strangers, to stay together (apart from deserting the odd member in the desert) and as such friction and factions began to appear.

Robbie and Julie had booked themselves into a cheap motel which cost about twenty five dollars and according to them, there was plenty of low rate accommodation to be had.

'I don't mind going overboard on me food, but I'll no' pay top dollar for me bed,' Robbie philosophised.

Readily taking his viewpoint to heart, I ordered an extra round of muffins and proposed we try and find an RV park. The RV park was easy to locate, I could see it on the top of a hill on the opposite side of the railway tracks. Of course there was a headwind for us to battle against and despite my best efforts it didn't appear to be getting any closer. After about twenty laborious minutes we arrived and I went up to the first trailer assuming it was the reception. I opened the screen and knocked on the door. No answer, so I knocked louder and shouted 'service'.

'Do you know,' said JK contemplatively, 'I don't think this is an RV park, I reckon it's a trailer park.'

I really could have done with knowing before shouting 'service' into someone's home. A rather scruffy looking guy pulled open the door. He was probably wondering what a scruffy looking guy was doing on his step.

I smiled and began, 'I wonder if you...'

He let the door slam shut. Resigned and repatriated, I pushed Corsair back up the driveway, then turned to see what was responsible for the weird rustling noise that was emanating from behind me. To my horror, a pit bull came tearing out from under the trailer. Shit! I panicked, I may have even squealed. Terrified, I couldn't coordinate my foot to clip into the pedal. I struggled and in doing so smacked my knee on the handlebars. Then at the last minute, I thrust Corsair between the slavering canine and myself. Simultaneously the dog was yanked to an abrupt halt with just a few feet to spare as its length of chain tightened. I tried to turn my cowardly move into a nonchalant stretch and even found the audacity to take a leisurely sip from my water bottle. I'm sure the shadowy figure behind the screen door saw through my machismo charade, and no doubt noticed my shaking hand and that I was trying to drink from an empty bidon.

I finally caught up with JK back on the right side of the tracks, he had turned and sprinted at around the time the rustling had started. After asking several people for directions we finally found a KOA campsite, which proved to be a little oasis in a rotten town.

'It's pretty windy out there today,' I commented to the receptionist whilst I was paying.

'It's always windy in Wyoming,' came her reply.

That explains why each tent pitch had a permanently erected windbreak.

The trail notes advised that the next town where groceries could be bought was not for another one hundred and thirty miles down trail at the skiing haven of Steamboat Springs. So once we had pitched our tent, we stuffed all of our gear inside and rode our unburdened bikes into Rawlings town centre. It was a strange experience riding Corsair without my unwieldy luggage attached. Rather than having the agility of an oil tanker – to which I had become accustomed – Corsair was light, frisky and responsive. Unfortunately, I couldn't get out of the habit of applying brute force and as such I continually over steered. Rather than look like the epic cyclist that I thought I had become, I resembled an old man faltering along the roadside on a bike he hadn't ridden for at least fifty years. By the time we arrived at the grocery store I was just getting the hang of it. But of course on the return journey I had grocery bags hanging off my handlebars which required brute force to operate. But now with my newly acquired lighter handling skills, I continually under steered and so adopted the faltering old man role once more.

That night in the tent whilst reading the trail notes by torch light, I learned the identity of the perpetrators of the large piles of manure at the trailside. Apparently they are called 'stud piles' and are deposited by wild stallions as a way of delineating their territory. I suppose the theory is, if a guy's shit is that big then you wouldn't want to mess with him. As I dozed off I wandered what the stallions would make of the stud pile I had left in the desert the previous day.

***

Day eighteen started with a pleasant little group ride out of town. We met up with Ronnie and Julie who had also adopted the early morning escape-the-heat philosophy and we all chatted for about an hour in our mini peloton. Our companions were finishing at Denver and as such they only had a couple of days left on the trail. They were happy to cruise along and savour the remaining experience. Of course, us being elite level cyclists, we didn't have time for all of this sightseeing, so we bid Ronnie and Julie farewell and pressed on with our important mission of setting records. You can imagine our embarrassment when they repeatedly caught us up every time we stopped for an essential food break. I could see that JK was becoming increasingly unsettled by this, to the extent that he enforced an eat-on-the-hoof policy until they were out of sight. Unfortunately our little cat and mouse game did little to take my attention off the energy sapping roller coaster terrain and the incessant Wyoming headwind.

The terrain was endless, tedious prairie comprising mainly scrub and sage bushes. But at least the fauna was far more interesting. All morning we encountered wild horses and pronghorns - an antelope type creature with a phenomenally quick turn of pace. To call a pronghorn an antelope is to do it an injustice because it is a unique animal that is not closely related to any other living creature on the planet. They display characteristics of other species such as giraffes, goats and sheep, but they have a trait that is unique to them. Instead of antlers which are shed annually, pronghorns have a bony horn that is covered with a sheath. They shed the sheath each year making them the only animals to do so. Even the wild horses in this area were special, as they are believed to be the descendants of horses brought to the New World in the sixteenth century by Spanish Conquistadors.

The timberless landscape abruptly gave way to aspens as we slowly climbed up to the Medicine Bow National Forest in the Sierra Madre mountain range. And at the same time the relatively flat terrain became an incline, which in turn morphed into a

83

gruelling, steep climb. The climbing got tougher and tougher as we inched our way up to Continental Divide crossing number twelve. As if to take my mind of the excruciating effort and the oppressive heat, there was an astonishing series of beaver ponds on my left. The way beavers have affected the landscape is remarkable, indeed it is purported that the only animals capable of altering the environment more than them is our own species. The beavers systematically build a series of dams across a stream with the intention of causing it to burst its banks and the resultant wetlands provide a safe underwater travel medium for them to access their favourite feeding grounds. The wetlands also enable new plants to thrive and attract insects and other wild animals including moose. When the old abandoned dams start to leak, the floodwaters drain away and the remaining land eventually becomes a meadow – and the meadows were truly beautiful. Admiring the scenery is all good and well, but it reminded me of a statement I had read in a mountain bike magazine. It went something like this: 'if you've got time to look at the scenery, you aren't working hard enough'. I wondered whether John Stamstad had the opportunity to ponder the ingenuity of a beaver dam. I think not. So as a nod of recognition towards professional cyclists everywhere, I decided to drop down a gear, stand on my pedals and crest the Continental Divide giving it one hundred and ten percent. Unfortunately, when I tried I found the task too difficult.

No matter where we have been, the toil of getting up to the Continental Divide has always been worth it. And in this case the victors got their spoils by way of a beautiful ride down the locally fabled 'Aspen Alley'. It is a mile long, off-road boulevard through a pristine aspen forest. Mountain biking is a unique experience in that the associated feelings of effort and exhilaration are juxtaposed to their extreme. On the climb up, I gave it my all; my legs felt heavy, my heart felt as though it was trying to fight its way out of my body via my mouth, sweat was stinging my eyes, I felt weak and Corsair's little nuances were really pissing me off. Moments later I was riding along Aspen Alley, feeding my soul on the beautiful surroundings and laughing at Corsair's trifling idiosyncrasies – the little scamp. And then I was fixing a puncture.

Storm clouds were gathering as I fitted a new inner tube, but their accumulating presence didn't bother me too much; according to the map, we only had a short ride to a campsite at a hamlet called Slater, situated on the Colorado border. Surprisingly the map was right and after a short ride on State Highway 70 we entered our fourth state and there was the campsite as promised. It was a rudimentary affair, but all we needed was a flat piece of ground, a toilet and some running water. And that is what we got - all for $5. The old woman, who was making a few bucks from renting out some of her field, invited us into her house while she laboriously filled out the paperwork for our paltry fee – she insisted on giving us a written receipt for the cash. While flicking through the guest book he was given to sign, JK noticed an entry from mutual friends of ours. It was strange to think that in 1997, Mark and Sally Fenner, who had ridden The Great Divide as their honeymoon, had found sanctuary in the very same field.

***

I suppose when you begin your journey at midday (like we had at Port Roosville), then technically Day One is only completed at midday the following day. The reason for the contrived mathematics was because John Stamstad finished the Great Divide in eighteen days and five hours. I was trying to buy us some time, but no matter how I cooked the books, the hard fact remained: if John Stamstad and I had started the ride together, he would have finished the ride on this day. Or put another way, it is on the nineteenth day that real cyclists finish the Great Divide. While I was trying in vain to find a statistical loophole, JK had developed a refreshing slant on our shortcomings.

'It just means that John Stamstad finished the ride earlier than us and that we are having to endure the hardship for longer than him,' he said in a tone that lead me to think he actually believed what he was saying, 'so really, he had it pretty easy.'

Ignoring the obvious naivety of his statement, I readily adopted the theory and used it as a very thin veneer to cover the overt fact that I was not a pro cyclist. Taking twice as long to do the ride means you're twice as macho. Right?

We were in Colorado and as if to underline the fact that the highest crossing of the Great Divide was in this state, the morning ride began with a thirty mile climb up to nine and a half thousand feet. The percentage of oxygen in the air at altitude is exactly the same as at sea level; the reason why breathing is difficult at altitude is because of the relative lack of atmospheric pressure. Or perhaps in this case it was due to a relative lack of fitness. The higher up you go the more the mercury in the barometer falls, and the harder it is to exercise. This is especially so for an habitual sea-level dweller like myself, and to make matters worse the last four miles of the climb had a profile not dissimilar to the exponential graph of my credit card interest.

Without warning the air changed from being thin, to overwhelmingly thick. Thick with the smell of death. I managed to keep pedalling whilst scanning for the source of this vile, gut-wrenching miasma. As I turned the corner the cause became apparent, a decomposing horse lay at the side of the trail, various animals had made a meal out of it and its carcass was contorted in an unceremonious way. I slowly crawled passed the remains, but due to my hypoxic state I was gulping in the putrid air. The summit couldn't have come soon enough; I pedalled slowly and breathed deeply in an attempt to purge my lungs of the fetid, nauseous gases.

An equally steep off-road descent ensued, which eventually joined a paved road at a small village named Clark. We stopped at the grocery store and I indulged myself with one of their wholesome turkey salad sandwiches and a bottle, of what was now obligatory, blue Gatorade. We sat on the veranda and ate our food whilst watching hummingbirds gorge themselves on hanging feeders. They are strange creatures, who seem to be missing the point: slow down. Their frenetic activity, which is chiefly eating whilst hovering, requires an inordinate amount of energy. Hummingbirds have to consume around two thirds of their bodyweight per day in order to fuel their feeding, which is a vicious circle. If only they realised that if they perched somewhere they wouldn't be expending vast quantities of energy and therefore wouldn't have to be continuously eating. Of course their plight is nowhere near as futile as my own. My ultimate aim is to end up at home – which is where I started – so if only I had realised that if I didn't cycle the Great Divide I wouldn't have had to consume the vast quantities of food that I did, and what's more it wouldn't have cost me a penny. On that hypocritical and edifying note, we cycled the remaining miles to Steamboat Springs.

CHAPTER EIGHT. STEAMBOAT SPRINGS TO MIDDLE OF NOWHERE

'we had entered high country'

These days Steamboat Springs is a world-renowned ski resort, but before the Norwegian Nordic ski champion Carl Howelsen moved into the area in 1913 and facilitated a skiing renaissance, it was also a well-established mining town. This dichotomy of new and old has lead to an interesting blend of demographics; skiers and mountain bikers mingle with Stetson wearing cowboys, and plush four-by-fours share parking lots with beaten up pickups. And smelly bikepackers share RV parks with well-to-do all-American families.

'What the hell kind of a two bit place is this?' bellowed an obese RVer at the campsite receptionist, 'when I say I want a full hook-up, I expect cable.'

It appears that to the archetypal American camper getting outdoors and being at one with nature requires a full hook-up. I'd seen the phrase 'FULL HOOK-UP' on billboards at previous campsites, but I had assumed it just meant electricity and water, not cable television as well. I couldn't help being staggered by the absurdity of it all; the majority of RVs are about the same size as an average English terrace house and the occupants drive it for miles, park up, watch cable television all day and cook on a gas barbeque. Why bother? Why not stay at home? But of course the same argument could be levelled at Great Divide riders – why bother?

We had the choice of two pitches and chose the one that was shaded by a large tree. Autonomously we set up camp and while we were contemplating what to have for our evening meal three mountain bikers hauling trailers rode past us heading for a small cluster of tents a couple of hundred yards away. We strolled over and introduced ourselves. They were a group of prospective Great Divide riders who were on a bikepacking preparation course run by Adventure Cycling. The leader of the group was an easy-going guy called Wally, who knew the rub. To call him an instructor would be to do him an injustice; I never noticed him instruct anyone, instead he advised his charges and encouraged experiential learning within the group. He was due to take the riders along the Great Divide trail for a couple of days, camping each night and then make the return journey over the following two days. The group comprised about ten riders of mixed ability, but they all had two things in common; they weren't short of a bob or two and they were extremely hospitable. The three returning riders had dragged trailers bulging with groceries intended for a meal that was to be staged later on that evening. JK and I now knew what our supper was going to be, we just had to sing for it. Without faltering we told embellished trail stories, hamming it up and exaggerating the facts as and when necessary. The food was delightful, it comprised fresh vegetable pasta, beer, and fruit and cream for dessert. As long as our stories flowed so too did the food. Needless to say we retired to our tent distended of stomach and hoarse of throat.

According to our map the terrain south of Steamboat Springs was generally upwards, which meant that we would soon enter the most elevated section of the ride – Indiana Pass territory. Because of this we decided that a preparation day would be a prudent move; we needed a rest and Vick and Corsair needed fettling before the challenging mountains tested our collective mettle. We went into town with a shopping list that comprised rubber and Calories; both of Vick's tyres and Corsair's rear tyre were bald, and we were both ravenous. The food was cheap enough, but purchasing the tyres was a similar ordeal to the shopping experience I had in Helena. I suppose it says a lot about the faceless capitalism a large population town breeds.

Back at the campsite, the vacant plot next to ours had been filled and the two bikes propped up next to the tent looked suspiciously like Robbie's and Julie's. We spent the afternoon milling around the campsite doing laundry, drinking tea, tweaking the bikes and just generally loafing. While we were having our evening meal, Robbie and Julie returned and joined us on the picnic table for a brew and a chat (if you're wandering about the fate of Vince, then let me allay your fears, according to Julie, who always had her finger on the trail-gossip pulse, he took a trail out of the desert before the A and M reservoir, arrived at Highway 789, came to his senses and called it a day). As the evening drew to a close a couple of cyclists with headlamps appeared out of the dusk. Rosy and Stuart had ridden intensely across the Basin. Being well and truly knackered they decided to take several rest days in Steamboat and had promised themselves a night on the town for a few well-earned beers. Unfortunately, we had an early start the next day and so had to abstain from the frivolities. It would have been nice to, but hey, these are the sacrifices a pro cyclist must make. However, I'm sure the glamorous life of a pro-cyclist doesn't involve sleeping in close proximity to something that sounds like an elephant bull seal's mating call.

'JK! Your snoring has got to stop mate, I'm going round the bend,' I said punching him out of his slumber.

'Shit! What the? Sorry mate,' came his groggy reply, 'I can't help it.'

'Well you're going to have to,' I countered sternly, 'from now on I'm operating a zero-tolerance policy, every time you wake me, I'll wake you.'

'Hay fever tablets help,' he said feebly.

'Well you'll have to get some,' I continued being fierce.

'Can the zero-tolerance policy start tomorrow?' he pleaded.

'NO!' I countered.

'Well I've got a few tablets in my bar bag, but they make me feel a little thirsty,' he said clicking his tongue as if for sympathy.

I handed him a drinks bottle.

***

The map profile for the ensuing day's ride looked like an 'M'. The first climb was a forty miler up to Lynx Pass at just under nine thousand feet followed by a second one up to Inspiration Point. The good news was that according to the trail notes Steamboat Springs is roughly halfway along the Great Divide trail and the prospect of finishing the route within our allocated time had for the first time begun to feel tangible.

Just to ensure that we didn't get too carried away, and to keep our delusions of adequacy in check, the sun put in its most gruelling appearance. On the drag up to Lynx Pass I felt an uneasy empathy with the ants I used to fry with a magnifying glass when I was a kid. We had a welcome rest and a chat when we caught up with Wally's Great Divide group, and their infectious enthusiasm for the route inspired us for the final eight mile grind to the summit. The terrain eased off and we wound along some beautiful, mellow mountain trails flanked with spruce and aspen. After about five miles we encountered a stream running across our path, known locally as Ford Rock Creek. It looked too deep to ride through so our only option was to carry the bikes across. As we sat on the bank deliberating the best way to approach the crossing a pseudo outdoorsman pulled up in a flimsy Japanese four-wheel drive. I say pseudo, because despite wearing all of the right gear, he looked out of place – sort of like a catalogue model. His matching supermodel wife also looked uneasy about the whole situation.

'How deep is it guys?' he asked standing up and looking over the windscreen.

'That's just what we were thinking,' JK replied.

'Let's turn back,' the supermodel interjected.

That would no doubt have been his first choice if they were alone. But to turn back would be a wounding blow to his ego, and heaven forbid, to turn back and let others attempt it would be fatal. JK had silently upped the ante; to him the victor had to be the first to cross the stream. He unlashed his baggage from Vick, held it aloft and waded across the stream. Did I say waded? Wrong word; even at the midway point the water barely reached his calves. Outdoorsman jumped into his seat and floored it across the stream sending a mini bow wave across JK's knees. Supermodel squealed with delight and hugged her alpha male as they raced off into the distance. JK was left despondently holding his gear above his head in a large puddle.

'JK, look out!' I shouted.

With a terrified look he turned around and with perfect timing I took a humiliating photograph. Well I would have if the camera batteries weren't flat.

Just as severely as we had gained altitude, we lost it. Within two miles we dropped 1500 feet through sun-baked tracks dotted with piñon and juniper. Descents are great but this one was a far cry from a Famous Five coasting with feet off the pedals affair. It was a bone shaking, muscle fatiguing, jarring lottery. Lactic acid seeped into my forearm muscles to the extent that I lost the feelings in them and couldn't tell whether I was applying the brakes or not. Nonetheless, the exhilarating scenery reminded me of that from a Sergio Leone spaghetti western, and for the remainder of the descent I indulged myself in the boyhood fantasy of being a cowboy, albeit on a titanium horse. We bottomed out with a crossing of the legendary Colorado River at a small place named Radium, which didn't even get a population mention on our map. Still perturbed by the fallout from my bad experience at Anaconda I was somewhat concerned about the origin of Radium. Apparently during the turn of the twentieth century, America had a love affair with all things radioactive due to the claimed restorative powers of disintegrating nuclei. Colorado was a major source of radium and in the spirit of the times, many towns and hot springs incorporated radium in their names, or claimed to be highly radioactive. Ironically a century later, nuclear power plants are doing the exact opposite.

At Radium we sat in a small car park next to the Colorado River and watched teams of college students race down the water on large tractor inner tubes. It looked great fun and if I hadn't been paralysed by a full body cramp I would have liked to have given it a try. A moment's carefree bliss in cool water would have been a tonic, instead we set about tackling the one thousand foot climb up to Inspiration Point, which in addition to being up was on an annoying northeast tack. It wasn't all bad though, the climb was on blacktop which meant it wasn't very technical, and I actually felt a wave of inspiration when I reached the Point and saw Kremmling (our destination for the night) at the base of a descent framed by the beginning of a magnificent sunset. We picked up the Transamerica Bicycle Trail once more and arrived in Kremmling late in the evening. Kremmling was a plain old American town that hadn't had the usual ski-town makeover. Some might say it was boring, but a staid, traditional settlement in beautiful surroundings was just what I needed. What's more the amenities were cheap.

After a gas station supper we checked in to Red Rock R.V. Park and pitched the tent on a small flat patch of grass that was also home to a child's swing, a climbing frame, a slide, and four other cyclists. After over twelve hours of cycling I forgot my manners and didn't even introduce myself to our new neighbours, instead I nodded vaguely in their direction, climbed into my sleeping bag and slept for six hours straight.

Since Steamboat the intensity had increased a few notches. The altitude and duration of the climbs were taking their toll on my body, and when I wasn't riding, I was either eating or sleeping. Day twenty two was no different and we started off with a drawn out forty mile climb up to Ute Pass which lingered at nine and a half thousand feet. At face value the climbing wasn't too bad, it was an agreeable, gentle incline alongside the Colorado River, meandering through the arid Williams Fork basin and then on up into Arapaho National Forest. But it was grinding, in a way that babysitting kids is; they're great for a couple of hours, but they wear you down over the long term. The same was true of the climb. There wasn't a section where I could pinpoint my steady decline into self-wallowing fatigue, instead it occurred little by little with each turn of the crank. A final series of false summits sapped the last bit of verve from my weary body and when I reached the top I knew I couldn't have climbed any further. Ooops, that was a false summit also, the real summit came half a mile later. The five mile descent moved the pain around in my body and allowed for a little respite. What's the old adage? "A change is as good as a rest." Instead of a searing pain in my legs and chest I now had it in my hands, lower back and neck as I rattled my way down to our good friend the Transamerica Bicycle Trail (a.k.a State Highway 9). Although I had earlier rebutted the Transamerica Bicycle Trail as a stretch of blacktop not worthy of a real mountain biker's itinerary, I relished the thought of its smooth, effortless, almost soothing surface. Oh how I paid for my hypocrisy. The currency was potholes more jarring than any I had encountered so far, and to make matters worse I was coerced Dual style by a juggernaut to ride it at full speed.

State Highway 9 was undergoing a resurfacing programme and as such the traffic was confined to one lane. A traffic light system was in operation orchestrating first the flow of northbound traffic and then southbound. However, unlike the British system (and I am in no way holding this method up as exemplary) of allowing small alternating aliquots of traffic through, the American system appears to let one set of traffic past for about half an hour before swapping over. The result is a tailback of several miles with the drivers' collective anger building up a huge head of pressure. Being on bikes we were able to saunter past the stationary traffic to the head of the queue where an attractive Hispanic woman, who looked out of place in workman's clothes, stood holding a STOP sign. No sooner had we arrived, she spun the sign around to reveal GO.

'Vaya con dios,' she said looking me dead in the eyes.

Vaya con what? A few feet behind a deafening air horn blew, signalling the start of a two mile death race.

Startled and fearing for my life I sprinted down the cratered road surface and just managed a quick glance over my left shoulder to see JK in a similar state of rattled shock. Just behind him a juggernaut was gaining like a big wave about to engulf an inept surfer. WOOOSH, the wing mirror of the truck flew past just inches from my left ear, dust was thrown into my face and the vortex caused by the vehicle rendered my attempts at steering arbitrary. I over steered to the right, clipped one, two, three, cones and then swerved back onto the potholed road just in time to have a close encounter with the tailgate of a pick up. The vehicles sped past as though we weren't there and those drivers that did acknowledge us did so in a less than friendly manner; they hollered and hooted their horns aggressively as though we had some other option. A momentary wave of relief washed over me when the last vehicle swept past and the stress immediately receded. That was of course, until I realised that as soon as our last car reached the end of the road works, a worker at the other end would reveal a GO sign and set another snarling pack of traffic upon us, only this time they would hit us head on. We had both simultaneously realised this and sprinted the remaining quarter mile like a couple of Tour de France riders battling it out on the Champs Elysee for a podium position. The last car cleared the road works about two hundred and fifty yards in front of us, and the worker operating the manual GO sign nodded towards us and seemed to be holding back the traffic as we raced towards the end. Then with about fifty yards remaining he spiced his otherwise dull day by turning the sign to GO. The driver of the lead pickup had seen us, but judging by his frenetic start we obviously weren't his problem; the worker had given him the carte blanche to tear up the strip and it was our responsibility to get out of the way. Instinctively we dived to our left and rode the remaining distance on hot sticky tarmac, which did nothing for our tyres, but cathartically did even less for their nice smooth road surface. That two mile sprint was one of the hardest I had ridden, and as a result I had to drop the pace and crawl into the next town, Silverthorne for some much needed refreshments.

As I have already mentioned, our maps were not the most detailed examples of cartography that I have seen, but one nice, informative touch is that the background colour ranged from green through to purple depending on the height of the terrain. Green was for lowlands with purple reserved for the mountainous areas. For the most part our maps had been varying shades of green, but when we changed maps at Silverthorne there was a distinct purple hue; we had entered high country.

Fighting the soporific effects of our refection, we left Silverthorne and headed for Breckenridge, our terminus twenty miles down trail. Thankfully we were spared State Highway 9 by an ingenious cycle route which had been built with a level of forethought and application that I have only seen equalled in Holland. It was light-years ahead of the British method of painting a token white line at the side of a congested, polluted main road. Although the route remained in close proximity to the highway, it meandered through scenic woodland, crossed purpose built wooden cycle bridges and was fun to ride. Sections of the route were adopted or sponsored by individuals, families or businesses and I was looking forward to arriving at Breckenridge if this was any indication of its forward thinking populous. Breckenridge certainly didn't disappoint. The streets were dotted with well kept Victorian houses, harking back to the prosperous days of the 1859 gold strike that occurred on the nearby Blue River. The town now reflects the more modern-day gold strike known as skiing. Breckenridge is one of the oldest towns in the state that has remained continually inhabited, the others are Aspen and Crested Butte both of which share a similar past and present with Breckenridge.

We were pointed in the direction of Fireside Inn by a local cyclist who recommended it as the best value-for-money digs in town. Fireside Inn was a cool, laidback hostel and we were greeted with the dulcet English voice of Andy Harris, the proprietor. He was the first English person we had met for a few days and I think it was the same for him. He swiftly set about making us feel welcome and offered us a pot of Twinnings Earl Gray tea and a copy of The Times. His appearance belied his past; he wore cut-off shorts, a faded T-shirt and a pair of sandals. In a former life he wore fatigues. Andy had had a distinguished career in the Army which spanned twenty six years, after which he did a few other odd jobs, before stumbling across the sale of the Fireside Inn whilst surfing the Internet for a skiing holiday. Andy and his wife Niki bought the Fireside Inn, moved to Breckenridge and have been successfully running it ever since. Our meagre budget stretched to a dormitory bunk each and we shared the room with Mick, an Australian snowboarder. Mick had recently flown over from the southern hemisphere in order to find a job for the upcoming ski season in an attempt to spend the winter snowboarding in Breckenridge. He was about as fiscally challenged as we were and allayed our fears of eating out in an expensive ski town. In his short time in

Breckenridge he had amassed an encyclopaedic knowledge of the best value eateries in town and so we decided to follow his advice and sample the Rasta Pasta restaurant. But before heading out I wanted to have a soak in the hot tub that I had seen advertised as being free to all Fireside Inn guests.

***

According to the map day twenty three was a purple one. Not in the sense of a purple patch, but in terms of altitude. The morning started with a fifteen mile climb to Boreas Pass, Continental Divide crossing number thirteen, at just under eleven and a half thousand feet. It wasn't as bad as it may sound because Breckenridge is situated at a rather elevated 9603 feet and the trail followed what was originally a wagon trail in the 1860s and later became the now abandoned narrow gauge Denver, South Park and Pacific Railway line. As such we were only dealing with locomotive grades, albeit rather relentless and circuitous ones. The railway line had begun in Denver and had been continuously extended south over Boreas Pass in 1881, and into Breckenridge by 1882. Finally the line was completed two years later when it reached the then silver boomtown Leadville.

The tracks have long since gone, but as we Amtraked our way up there was plenty of evidence that locomotives had made the same laborious route over a century earlier. One such remnant was Baker's tank, a wooded cistern that was used as a water reserve for the steam driven locomotives. It was here that we met Paul, a local trailhound. He lived in Breckenridge and had been meaning to do the Great Divide ever since Drew Walker first completed the route back in 1997.

'Fuckin'-A dudes,' he drawled in a surfer–like manner, 'man, I've always wanted to do it, but I just can't find the time.'

I mentioned something about having to find the time and how important it is to do these things. I also glossed over the fact that when I was living in West Sussex and the South Downs Way passed my back door, I never got round to riding it despite it being at the top of my to-do list. I had to wait five years and move over three hundred miles away before I finally got my act together and rode it.

Paul rode with us for a while but soon became out of breath and turned off to ride some good looking single-track. It was good to have a new rider as a yardstick; JK and I had obviously been getting fit together and as such no relative improvement was evident. But to beat a local who was not laden with kit was a nice boost to my confidence and took the sting out of the final push to the summit. Even the trains had a tough time of it towards the top of the climb; folklore has it that when P.T. Barnum's circus train ground

94

to a halt on the pass, they let the elephants out of their carriages and got them to lend a helping push.

Boreas Pass is the highest Continental Divide crossing and is the second highest climb of the Great Divide. Although it had taken a long time to get to the top, it boded well for tackling Indiana Pass, which is only 428 feet higher. Apparently in the railway's heyday the summit used to be a hive of activity, with Boreas station having the highest post office in the entire United States. Fortunately there was no sign of Boreas, the Greek god of the North Wind when we rode the ten mile descent to Como in beautiful mountain stillness. Italian settlers named it Como after its doppelganger in Northern Italy. It proved to be a little oasis comprising of nothing more than a mercantile and the Como Depot Restaurant. Fancying a light lunch, I ordered a decaf and a grilled ham and cheese sandwich. Only it wasn't grilled and it wasn't light. I suppose the proprietor was only being kind in a motherly sort of way; on seeing our emaciated waif-like appearance it is only natural to assume that we needed filling up. In addition the typical somatotype in this state was skewed heavily towards the endomorph, which no doubt will have exaggerated our feeble demeanour. Either way the toast for my sandwich was fried to such an extent that it redefined how much oil a slice of bread can absorb. The processed cheese was stacked ten slices thick and the entire contents of a wafer-thin ham packet made up the meat. It was a towering fat sandwich. Of course I ate it and enjoyed it so much that I was unable to help JK finish off the cherry pie that he had ordered between us. The doorbell jangled and a couple of regulars waddled in. I knew straight away that they were regulars because they had seamlessly adapted their massive girths to negotiating the four stairs leading down from the door; they edged their way sideways with both hands on the banister. At least I now knew how I was going to make my rotund exit.

Fully fed and with our water bottles and drinking bladders refilled we headed off for Hartsel, which according to the map symbol was home to either a motel, a hotel, or a bed and breakfast. The whole area is known as South Park as in the South Park cartoon, yet it has little in common with its animated namesake. That is apart from a few weird characters in Hartsel. The main mercantile in most villages, as you would imagine, is a vital lifeline for the remote communities it serves. In most instances these have been little godsends where we have been able to stock up on essential day-to-day items, you know, like food. I knew things were going to be a little strange when the shop window was full of inflatable aliens and expensive irreparable 1920s police toys. What kind of a community demands these knickknacks from its mercantile? I stayed outside with the

95

bikes and JK went inside for supplies. I took a few photographs whilst I was waiting, and when I was composing one particular shot a Dukes of Hazard car pulled up into my viewfinder. A Deliverance extra appeared out of nowhere and the two characters shiftily exchanged a few items. It was around about then that they noticed I was pointing my camera at them and rapidly dispersed. What were they exchanging? Moon dust? Or perhaps black-market 1920s police cars. Either way I didn't want to find out.

'Christ it was weird in there,' JK commented, 'the guy said he didn't know if there was anywhere to sleep. You would think in a place this small you'd know.'

We decide to push on and try our luck finding a camp spot further up the trail. From Hartsel we rode two miles, for the last time, on the Transamerica bicycle Trail before the route took us over a barren basin that rose up towards the San Isabel National Forest.

Ute Indians were the first humans in South Park. They lived off the land and hunted the numerous bison and elk that roamed the area. Spanish explorers, gold prospectors, and demented mountain bikers then followed their footsteps. The natural salt springs in the area were capitalised and the Colorado Salt Works sprang into action, which was capable of producing two tons of salt a day. The salt was used for culinary purposes but it was also used in the gold mining industry, as it is an essential ingredient for refining gold ore.

The bison were long gone and all we had to eat were chocolate bars. I bit into a Snickers and immediately spat it out; it was rotten. I went to take a sip from drinking bladder but all I got was resistance. When scuba diving the realisation that you've run out of air only hits you after an exhalation; your next inhalation is met with opposition and the realisation that your lifeline has been cut off. It was a similar experience, but with less dramatic consequences. The foul taste in my mouth wasn't the problem. What I was concerned about was that we were twelve miles into the arid basin and I was without water, and upon inspection, JK only had a cup's worth. It was getting late and we needed to set up camp soon. We had two options: retrace our tyre tracks back to Hartsel and try our luck finding a bed in the strange town, or push on into the dusk for another forty five miles towards Salida and hope that there was some surface water before then. We chose the latter.

It's a strange situation to be in, cycling into the unknown yet knowing that with each pedal stroke we were getting further away from Hartsel - a definite water source. We picked up the pace because our worse case scenario was to have to ride all of the way to Salida. Daylight was rapidly running out and, not having any cycle lights, we didn't want to have to navigate this terrain in the dark. Getting lost could easily have had serious ramifications and my mind turned once again to the ants that I had fragged. Luckily I was buoyed by a house-like silhouette on the horizon and upped the pace dreaming of faucets and cool water. You can imagine my surprise when the silhouette morphed into a pronghorn and ran off into the distance. I was therefore sceptical about the next house shape that presented itself, but as we got closer its structural form became apparent. We pulled into the lot and a hosepipe was conspicuously lying in front of the house. A hermit appeared in the doorway and was hospitable to our requests for water. He disappeared inside and turned the tap on. Crystal clear water poured from the pipe and within minutes our water caches were fully bloated.

With our only worry allayed, we set up camp half a mile down the trail. It is amazing how one minute things could be so desperate and then because of a tap – which we all take for granted – there was an about turn and things were back on track. In possession of an abundant water supply we threw caution to wind and re-hydrated an extra powdered meal each. What the hell we had cause for celebration.

CHAPTER NINE: MIDDLE OF NOWHERE TO DEL NORTE

'climbs cannot go on forever'

I was feeling the effects of camping at altitude whilst having breakfast. The dawn air was cold and being a sea level dweller it appeared thin to me. So thin in fact that I was breathless just eating my breakfast; to swallow food was to miss out on breathing, which then meant I was playing oxygen debt catch-up for the next few breaths. Fortunately I habitually approach my breakfast more energetically than I do my cycling.

As a result of being in the mountains, I had made psychological changes as well as, or to counteract, the sliding physiological ones. I had changed my distance reference from the horizontal to vertical. When we started the Great Divide I had been solely concerned with how far we had ridden and calculated our progress as a fraction of the total distance we had to cover. What was of greater importance in the mountains was how high we were; being at ten thousand feet meant that we still had about two thousand vertical feet to go before reaching the apex of the route. We also paid a lot more attention to the profile legends on the map. That was of course until they repeatedly let us down. Having ascended relentlessly for over thirty miles, according to the map, we had completed all of the climbing for the day and should have been enjoying a nice flat ridge before descending into a little town called Salida. But the reality was different: we were faced with a one thousand foot climb, and of course there was nothing we could do to alter this reality. Telling the climb that it shouldn't be there wasn't going to make it vanish, nor was yelling at the map going to help. The only solution was to shut up and keep pedalling. During the previous days our progress in the mountains had been pedestrian at best or pathetic at worst, and the best way I could mentally deal with the climbs was to watch the altimeter on my cycle computer slowly nudge its way up to the known spot height at the summit. Throughout the ascent I would tell myself 'you're a quarter of the way there...a third of the way there...half way there' and so on. I can tell myself the best of lies (remember the one about being a pro cyclist?), but to tell yourself that according to your altimeter and the map you're at the top even though the trail continues to wind upwards before your eyes is not an easy one, and indeed I failed miserably. I swapped this mental torture for a more pragmatic approach; I was at the top when all trails go downhill.

Despite painful protestations from my legs, I rationalised that climbs cannot go on forever and as we rose through aspen groves and past rocky outcrops, logic eventually prevailed and we crested the ostensible climb. Although the views were rewarding, I was still pissed off with the cartographers. To my west were the impressive Collegiate Peaks: Mount Harvard, Mount Columbia, Mount Yale, and Mount Princeton. These mountains form part of the Sawatch Range and are members of the elite group of "14ers", so called because they exceed fourteen thousand feet. There are fifteen peaks in the Sawatch Range that qualify as 14ers, and an impressive non-collegiate one is Shavano Peak, named in honour of Chief Shavano, the head honcho of the Tabeguache Utes. We had arrived too late in the season to see the full ethereal effects of the snowfields that melt on its flanks. Apparently as they recede they resemble an angel with outstretched arms and folklore has it that the apparition is the annual return of the angel that used to visit the Chief during his prayers.

Although cycling up these ascents was an uncomfortably hot and sweaty process, the descents through the thin mountain air were chilling, especially when wearing sweat-drenched clothes. So I donned my Mountain Equipment windproof jacket and prepared for the downhill re-entry into the lowlands. The drop down into Salida was as dramatic as they come; nearly three thousand vertical feet in about twelve miles. The thirty minute descent proved to be a displacement oxymoron. In the bottom left hand corner of my cycle computer screen the odometer was silently clocking up the miles indicating a forward advancement along the route, whereas in the bottom right corner the altimeter was falling with alarming speed indicating, in a vertical sense, that I was going backwards.

Salida proved to be an oxymoron as well; it was an historically modern town. As with most towns in this area of Colorado, the Ute Indians originally settled here and their presence remains in the names of the local mountain peaks. The familiar influx of the usual suspects ensued with explorers, miners, railroad developers, farmers and ranchers all trying their luck in Salida and as a result it became a quintessential Wild West town. Although the inhabitancy of these early settlers has receded over the years they have left their mark. As we rode through downtown Salida I was impressed how the old red brick buildings that once were thriving bordellos and bars were now tastefully converted into cafes, restaurants and art shops. Of course statements like that need to be backed up, and it was with vigour that I patronised several of the local businesses – the cafés of course, not the bordellos! Sitting at a window seat, munching my tuna steak sandwich, sipping my coffee and watching the new and old world go by I decided that Salida was my favourite town so far; there was something cool about the place. And then the bill arrived.

'Looks like were camping again tonight; no motel for us,' JK commented looking at the tariff.

We pitched up at Salida campsite just as some ominous storm clouds were gathering overhead.

'Looks like it's going to rain,' JK said to the receptionist whilst he was paying for the pitch.

'It never rains in Salida,' came her confident reply.

I would like you to remember those words.

We pitched the tent under the gaze of a fellow camper and once we had sorted ourselves out, he came over and introduced himself.

'Hi, I'm Keith, you doin' the Divide?' he said offering us a couple of bottles of beer, 'thought you might be needing a drink,' he added.

He wasn't wrong.

Keith was a middle-aged guy who had decided to ride sections of the Great Divide in no particular logical order. It was his inaugural section and he had chosen the steepest. He had teamed up with some friends who had been riding progressive sections for the last few years and was joining them in a couple of days. He intended to get all of his training done in the next forty eight hours. He slapped his paunch and commented, 'I should be okay, fancy another beer?'

Marshall Pass, tomorrow's two and a half thousand foot climb, loomed over the campsite and we stood in quite contemplation looking at the formidable mountain whose summit was shroud in storm clouds.

'Looks like it's going to rain,' I said to Keith.

'It never rains in Salida,' came his confident reply.

I would like you to remember those words.

***

It wasn't raining too hard when we broke camp the following morning. That only happened when we rode out of town on Federal Highway 285. It was short lived. The highway that is, not the rain. We turned onto a dirt track and the intensity of the downpour increased concomitantly with the incline. To be riding in the driving rain was somehow reassuringly familiar, it reminded me of summer riding back home. There's an old adage in Mawsnram, India – the world's wettest inhabited place – that goes: there's no such thing as bad weather, just the wrong clothes. That morning I was feeling particularly smug, I was wearing my super waterproof, super breathable Patagonia jacket, and my clean, dry spare clothes were protected from the elements in my waterproof Ortlieb sausage bag. It was one of those two-fingers up to the weather situations, like on a cold Sunday morning with the rain lashing at your bedroom window and you're safely cocooned under your duvet.

'John, you might want to duct tape that rip in your bag,' JK advised nodding at my sausage bag, 'looks like it's leaking pretty bad.'

I craned my neck to look and a pool of rainwater that had been gathering in a jacket crease was unleashed sending cold rivulets down my back. Then Corsair's chain fell off.

While I was sticking two fingers up at the weather, fate was giving me the middle finger in the form of my cycle rack rubbing a hole in my waterproof bag. My cosy Sunday morning had become a detestable Monday. Wet, annoyed and covered in an inordinate amount of chain oil I remounted Corsair and vowed not to show that kind of disrespect to the elements again. Desperate, I decided to believe in karma for the rest of the mountain stage in a way that an atheist who has got something bad on the horizon begins cutting deals with God. 'Just let me get through the mountains and I'll eat all of my greens forever.'

The ride over Marshall's Pass followed the old Denver and Río Grande Railroad whose tracks were laid in 1881. The convoluted, easy grade trail meant that it was a long drawn out process getting to the top. Because it was an old railroad bed the riding wasn't very technical and as such it didn't require much concentration. This meant that my idling mind was free to wander, and having latched on to the words Río Grande, it wasn't long before it threw up Duran Duran's 'Rio' song.

Without warning I broke into the first line of the chorus, *'her name is Rio and she dances on the sand,'* and then I drew a blank. I began humming the rest when JK shot me an evil glance as though, in forgetting the lines, I had mortally wounded him. And with an arrogant air of confidence he sang the remainder, *'just like a Rizla clubbing through my rusty mind.'*

His lyrics seemed somewhat questionable but with nothing better to go off, and with JK's supreme confidence in them being kosher, we sang those two lines on a loop for the remainder of the twenty five mile climb. My old recorder teacher used to tell 1C that practice makes perfect. Well she was wrong, practice makes permanent. And after having sung those spurious lyrics repeatedly for over an hour and half they, whether correct or incorrect, became laser etched into my temporal lobe. I think the Germans call it an earworm or something like that.

Marshall's Pass was our fourteenth crossing of the Continental Divide and standing proud at 10,842 feet it was within spitting distance of Indiana Pass' loftiness.

101

We were so close to the highest point of the whole ride, but unfortunately the next twenty miles were a steady decline alongside Marshall Creek to a village called Sargents. "Elevation High, Population Few" read the welcome sign to Sargents, but I found the Gas Station sign more convivial because it meant garage food and decaf. We stocked up with the usual candy bar trail food there and headed next door to a café-cum-bar for our decaf fix. The door was open, but a sign which read "closed on Sundays" was tacked onto the doorframe. There was no body inside until the guy who had served us at the gas station walked in and assumed the role of bar tender.

'Can I have a couple of decafs?' I inquired.

'Can't you read the sign?' he said chuckling to himself.

'Yeah, it says you're shut on Sundays,' I replied trying to work out what day it was. I added, 'what day is it?'

'Saturday,' he replied smiling.

'Okay, so I should be able to order a decaf.'

'Nope.'

'Why not?'

'Because we only sell fully leaded,' he said laughing out loud.

The conversation was getting a touch surreal, and I turned to JK for a bit of moral support but found he had joined in with the histrionics and was having a good laugh at my expense.

'Okay, can I have a couple of regular coffees?' I gingerly inquired.

'No problem, I will put a fresh pot on for you,' he said and headed out the back to the kitchen.

We took a seat at a table and spread out the maps. The comical bar tender brought over our coffees and informed us that they have a free refill policy. He pulled up a chair and quizzed us about the ride. Despite our initial interaction I warmed to him and his unique brand of sarcastic humour. A couple of bikers stuck their heads around the door.

'You guys open?' the larger of the two asked.

'Can't you read the sign?' said the bar tender standing up and returning to the bar.

'Yeah, it says you're shut on Sundays, it's Saturday right?'

'Yep,'

'So you're open.'

'Yep.'

After three refills I was feeling the effects of a caffeine buzz, which I am sure was responsible for reducing my tolerance to the non-funny joke the bartender went through for each and every customer. What was only meant to be a pit stop had turned into a coffee drinking, people watching afternoon off, and much later than we had initially intended we set off on Federal Highway 50 to Doyleville, which was on a non-productive westerly tack. It was about a thirteen mile ride from Sargents to Doyleville, and despite this paltry distance, the flat blacktop and the rain stopping, it was a crippling ride for us both. I am sure the caffeine was responsible; after four full strength coffees following weeks of abstinence our bodies were well and truly screwed. We turned off the road at Doyleville and as the grade increased we decided to – no, had to – call it a day. We had only covered fifty five miles and it was becoming apparent, just like it does in the Tour de France, that the mountains are where a cyclist's mettle is tested; you have to be fully prepared and show them respect. On John Stamstad's record setting ride he had completed between 130-190 miles each day, no double figure days for him. Our low standards and lack of professionalism were becoming apparent and we both knew it. Things had to change.

***

Our chastising was still fresh in our minds the following morning. We were two days off tackling Indiana Pass and we needed to get our shit together if we were going to make good progress through the mountains. We were at a crucial stage, and the following few days at altitude would determine whether or not we would be on schedule for finishing the Great Divide.

Getting up at 5.00 am is never good for morale, nor is eating re-hydrated cardboard-oatmeal for breakfast, but I was determined to have a positive, professional cyclist's outlook. I took my mind off the gruel by watching JK lance his bubble wrap boil on the sole of his foot. I stared with morbid fascination as he jabbed his penknife blade deep into the pustule, causing its contents to be spewed out. Then, to my horror, I realised he was sitting on my sleeping bag.

'Christ JK, you could have done it on your own bag!' I shouted spraying cardboard oatmeal everywhere.

'Shit, sorry mate. You can have my sleeping bag,' he offered, in some form of compensatory tone.

It was a zugzwang; his bag had taken on an unwashed waxy sheen.

'No, it's alright mate,' I replied, 'just clean it up with a baby wipe please.'

I thought I was dealing well with these impediments to my newfound positive outlook, until I checked out the profile for the day: another relentless, bastard of a climb, this time up to Cochetopa Pass. The profile was a series of rollers which, over forty miles, rose over two thousand vertical feet to the pass - our fifteenth Continental Divide crossing. Cochetopa is Ute for buffalo crossing and the pass was an important route across the Continental Divide for the Indians. It later proved irresistible to the entrepreneurial Otto Mears and Enos Hotchkiss, who in 1870 built a toll road along it and monopolised this vital passage. John Fremont and his group subsequently used it during their reconnaissance expeditions for the transcontinental railroad route and it was in these parts that the group's guide became disorientated and they all became lost. This is unforgiving country and as a result of a severe blizzard almost a third of the thirty five strong party perished. In the early twentieth century the pass was tamed somewhat and following the popularity of the internal combustion engine, it was improved and opened to cars.

JK was fully aware of the requirements and repercussions of the next few days and set about the climb with a steely determination. Indeed it was almost as if Vick could sense that it was not the time to mess about and even he obediently settled down to his mechanical duties. Corsair on the other was insubordinately protesting against the toil with alarming metal-on-metal noises which seemed to be emanating from the rear wheel, yet they were transient and hard to locate. As the ascent continued, the metallic decibels increased. I re-lubed the chain which helped for a while, but after a short respite the screeching was back with greater vengeance. I was also getting feedback from the drive chain, which led me to believe that the rear cassette (the series of concentrically smaller cogs on the rear wheel) was knackered. In my newfound positive frame of mind I felt confident that it would hold out for another sixty four miles until we reached Del Norte where there was, according to the map, a bicycle shop. Christ I was even being positive about the map!

We dropped down from the Pass losing two thousand vertical feet in about ten miles and entered a landscape rich in cactus, red rock outcrops and Spanish influence. We joined State Highway 114 for a few miles before turning south back onto a dirt road that meandered its way up a spectacular canyon in the La Garita Mountain range. After a short distance we entered the Río Grande National Forest to the Pavlovian chorus:
'Her name is Rio and she dances on the sand,
Just like a Rizla clubbing through my rusty mind.'
If we hadn't turned off and ridden a few more miles east along Highway 114 we would have encountered the town of Saguache (Indian for Blue Earth), which also had a dodgy association with cannibalism. Legend has it that in January 1874 Alfred Packer and several other prospectors from Utah had headed into the San Juan Mountains in search

of gold. Ouray, the Ute chief of the time advised them not to head into the mountains due to the ferocity of the winter, yet despite this inauspicious warning the prospectors were drawn by the lure of gold and making a fast buck. As predicted, the winter that year was particularly harsh and the prospectors became trapped high up in the mountains. It wasn't until the following spring that Alfred wandered into town and, not being the cleverest of cannibals, he aroused suspicion with the locals after he was spotted in a saloon spending large amounts of cash from several different wallets. He claimed that whilst being trapped in the mountains his companions had died fighting amongst themselves and that he had been forced to kill one man in self-defence, and in order to survive he had eaten the corpses' flesh. The following summer five dead bodies were found. Four of the men had been bludgeoned to death and the fifth had been shot in the head. All of them had flesh removed from their chests and thighs - presumably for consumption by Packer. Packer was initially sentenced to the gallows but his conviction was overturned and he was convicted of manslaughter. Nobody really knows for sure whether Packer cannibalised his companions but in 1989 the bodies of the five prospectors were exhumed and forensically analysed. It was concluded that he had indeed eaten their flesh. You would think a town would try and play down this deplorable act, but no not Saguache; apparently any claim to fame is better than none.

The unforgiving mountain routine thrust one tall piece of earth at us each day, and that was about all we could manage. As the trail wound itself upwards towards the next helping of mountain – Carnero Pass – a timely primitive campsite, known locally as Big Springs Picnic site appeared at the trailside, marking the end of the day's toil. We had set up camp at about six o'clock which was relatively early, so we had a bit of time to prepare a warm meal rather than the hotchpotch of snacks we usually ate whilst pitching the tent. JK cooked a soup and dehydrated potato mix. The potato mix was a deluxe four cheese variety and the resultant concoction was very palatable (you must bear in mind that my palate and taste buds had rotted away as a result of the highly refined sugar diet that I had been living on). To be honest anything that wasn't chocolate or fig based would have tasted good. We even had the time for a couple of brews and some finger nibbles in the form of a crushed box of Ritz crackers. I eased myself into my sleeping bag and prayed that the cleaning properties of a baby wipe were sufficient to kill any of the nasties that had spewed out of JK's foot boil. Surprisingly I managed to have a good night's sleep.

***

105

Back in Steamboat Springs I had censured Wendy about calling The Great Divide a holiday. Yes, it was hard work back then, but it was also great fun. The fun element, although still an ingredient, was far less obvious during a morning in the mountains; it was always cold, we were always knackered and breathless and there was the ubiquitous knowledge that the subsequent hours were going to be spent toiling upwards. Nonetheless as each day passed, so too did a major climb.

A mile and a half after cresting Carnero Pass the trail notes read: 'Beautiful surroundings of boulders and hoodoos.' And sure enough the area was breathtaking, but it is certainly worth commenting on the ambiguity of hoodoo. The North American understanding of the word is a pillar of rock that is a weird shape and sure enough in front of me were many examples of that. Or there is the alternative interpretation of hoodoo, which is regarded as a malign influence that prevents you achieving winning form in a sport, and there were also two knackered examples of that at the top of the pass. We had got the timing correct climbing Carnero Pass (or more accurately, it was probably down to the law of averages) and got to the summit before the sun had reached its zenith and the temperature escalated. We opted to skip our scheduled snack break, mainly because we'd had enough of the refined confectionery and our stomachs were balking at the mere thought of a candy bar. But also because our only bag of trail mix was curry flavour which didn't do much for our stomachs, nor could it be buffered at the other end with nappy cream. Also in our favour was a twenty mile downhill to a small village called La Garita which proudly sported a knife and fork on our map. A sunny descent in beautiful scenery ending with real food in La Garita – perfect. I took my fingers of Corsair's brake levers, stood on the pedals and let gravity take over. In parts the trail was wide allowing me to reach speeds of up to thirty five miles per hour, in others it was narrow and technical and was fun to ride, and of course in others it corrugated washboards which required a lot of pedalling despite going downhill. We were following the gully eroded by the Canero Creek and six miles outside of La Garita, at Coolbroth Canyon, we were treated to the Gates of the Canyon – a passageway through huge impressive columns of basalt, accompanied by a grating metallic chorus from Corsair's cassette.

La Garita is a couple of miles off the official Great Divide route, but where food is concerned I don't mind putting in an extra four mile round trip. The area around La Garita is rich in history, especially nearby Penitente Canyon where there are wheel ruts gouged into the rock; a reminder of the numerous horse drawn wagons that once used the trail. The canyon is named after Los Hermanos Penitentes who were a faction of the

Catholic Church brought to the New World from Europe in the late sixteenth century. The cult religious group was originally confined to just New Mexico, but a century later sects had found their way into southern Colorado. As part of their extreme practices worshipers would perform self-flagellation and other torture rituals – the worst having to be the re-enactment of the crucifixion of Christ by actually nailing members to the cross and leaving them there until they passed out. But what I found most amazing was these activities were still being performed well into the twentieth century.

As soon as the café sign came into view I was salivating. As soon as the "We're closed on Mondays" sign came into view I was crying. Writing for www.airborne.net, Dave Thiess commented that as a motivational tool 'John [Stamstad] would pick places on the map and mentally work on arriving at that point'. I had a similar philosophy only mine always had a gastronomic slant. I would pick a place on the route – in this case the knife and fork symbol at La Garita – and promise myself an abhorrent amount of food in return for my legs getting me there. My legs had kept their half of the bargain and to have their reward taken away at the last minute was devastating. Fuck being positive, I was really pissed off. Under these conditions, the two mile return journey back to the trail was a chore that grated with every pedal stroke. To make matters worse the trail swung through ninety degrees on a due east tack and put us straight into a headwind. I was extremely fatigued and was on the verge of bonking, but I wasn't so bad that I would risk attempting the curry flavoured trail mix. Mercifully the trail had another ninety degree kink and it sent us south on a very primitive trail. This stretch of single-track was undoubtedly the best we'd ridden so far on the Great Divide. It was ever so slightly down hill and was twisty and technical and above all it was fast and fun. It goes to show that fatigue is largely a mental issue because I was actually disappointed when the six mile trail finished and spat us out in Del Norte.

Del Norte with its population of 1,674, was the biggest town we had been in since Salida and it had a full services star. We weren't in a hurry and so we decided to eat first before attempting to fix Corsair's cassette. No sooner had that decision been made and we were standing in a queue at a burger bar. I rattled off my extensive choice of food to JK and left him in the queue whilst I reconnoitred the town for a bike shop. I asked a local lad on a BMX if he knew where the bike shop was and he directed me to a hardware-cum-cyclery.

'I don't suppose you've got a nine speed XT cassette, have you?' I asked the elderly gentleman behind the counter.

He tilted his head and gave me one of those say what? looks.

'Or a cassette cracker tool?'

Same response.

Okay, it was time to backtrack and start from the ground up.

'My mountain bike is broken. I think the cog on the back wheel has worked loose. Do you have any spares, or a tool I can use to tighten it up?'

'All of the bike stuff is hung up on that board over there,' he said pointing to a distant isle. I followed his directions but couldn't see any bike spares. I stopped in front of a child's whitewall bike tyre, a horn and a handlebar mirror that were zip tied onto a drilled out piece of plywood.

'Whereabouts did you say?' I inquired.

'You're looking at it,' came the condescending tone.

Back at the burger bar JK had attracted the attention of a couple of cycle enthusiasts and between bites of burger, he was telling them the usual trail stories. I eschewed the conversation in favour of Calories and only when my blood sugar had resumed to normal levels could I hold an adult conversation without bursting into tantrums. One of the cyclists, Dave, was only in Del Norte working; he lived thirty miles out of town. He offered to pick up the tool I needed from home and bring it back to Del Norte later on that evening. I took him up on his kind offer and told him I would meet him at the local campsite, but I didn't for one minute think he would show up.

On route to the Woods and River R.V. Park we passed a gas station where I picked up a can of WD40. Knowing what a cure-all it is for any mechanical problem I thought it might help bring Corsair back to life. While JK pitched the tent I set about spraying the entire contents of the can on Corsair's cassette with all of the enthusiasm, but sadly without the artistic flare of graffitist. WD40 is a very thin oil which readily displaces heavier oil, grime and dirt and I was amazed by the amount of crap that fell out of the cassette. After giving Corsair a trial lap of the campsite I diagnosed him cured and tossed the can into a nearby bin feeling very smug about my mechanical prowess. Then I noticed Dave approaching. He had driven a sixty mile round trip just to bring me a cassette tool. Two waves of guilt washed over me: one for doubting him and two for not having a faulty cassette.

'How's the bike?' he asked.

'Still knackered,' I replied, shocking myself at the lie I was telling. Somewhere a subconscious part of my brain was taking over; I had no option but to go along for the ride.

'Well let's have look,' he said, relishing a bike mending session.

'NO, NO, NO!' I shouted, startling us both, 'I'll do it; it's a little fiddly with English bikes you see,' I blurted, hoping he didn't notice the blatant "Handmade in the USA" sticker on the top tube, or that Shimano – the manufacturer of the cassette – is a well known globalised Japanese company. Either way, probably out of fright, he let me tighten the cassette. Of course the cassette was as tight as the day I had put it on, but my audience wanted to see it tightened - he hadn't driven sixty miles not to see a show. With some deft hand movements I managed to feign a quarter turn with the spanner, but unfortunately I didn't fake the bit were the spanner slipped and I raked my knuckles across the teeth of the cogs.

'Let's have a look,' Dave asked.

So I handed him the wheel.

'Yep, you've done a good job of tightening that,' he commented.

I basked in the praise and said, 'well when you're on the trail as long as I am you've got to make sure everything's tight otherwise,' and to add a bit of drama I drew my forefinger across my throat.

Dave then added, 'but which stupid twat has covered your wheel in oil, you'll never be able to brake.'

CHAPTER TEN: DEL NORTE TO PLATORO

'if I just stopped pedalling'

'Fittingly, getting to Indiana Pass is no picnic,' JK commented, reading aloud from the trail notes.

'Extra oatmeal for breakfast then?' I inquired, and emptied another couple of sachets of the cardboard-gruel into the morning cookpot.

'It says here that you won't forget the final twelve miles up to the Pass,' he added in a sadistic tone, as if to suggest he was just going to watch me suffer rather than ride it himself. Or maybe he was just gunning for even more oatmeal, I wasn't sure. Slightly perturbed I traced the day's map profile with my finger. The first twelve miles seemed reasonably flattish – hovering around eight thousand feet – and then it abruptly went up; in twelve short miles we would have to climb nearly four thousand vertical feet. A succinct footnote read: "Get an early morning start out of Del Norte, because you've got a huge climb ahead". I poured the remainder of our sachets into the gruel.

We topped off our water supplies and set off out of Del Norte alongside Pinos Creek to begin our unceremonious wrestle against gravity. It seemed a good day to tackle Indiana Pass because there was a lot of cloud cover that had fortuitously rendered the heat bearable. The first dozen miles slipped under our tyres fairly easy and we cruised along under a mackerel sky in high, albeit nervous spirits. After all, Indiana Pass is, to Great Divide riders, what Mount Ventoux is to Tour de France cyclists. Mount Ventoux, the worlds windiest place, is one of the most storied climbs in the Tour de France and is revered by cyclists the world over. It is an arduous, twenty one kilometre climb taking the competitors to the hostile, barren summit which resides at just over 6200 feet. It is the place where races are won or lost, careers are made or broken, heroes are forged or losers scorned. It is also the place were legendary British cyclist Tom Simpson collapsed and died as he struggled to tackle the summit back in the 1967 Tour de France. Our analogous climb, to be honest, seemed quite easy in comparison. That it to say it was, up until the point where it became really difficult. At this point our conversation abruptly halted and my breathing became laboured; somebody somewhere had accidentally leant on the gravity dial and moved it to the FULL ON position. The gradient kept getting tighter and my notions of having served my apprenticeship and earned real cyclist status vaporised in front of my eyes and once more I slumped into the ungainly head-on-the-bar bag position. My over strained body was going through its now well-rehearsed energy saving protocol:

'Shut down all conversation.' 'Check'.

'Cut off peripheral vision centre.' 'Check'. And with that I receded into a lonely, distant, tunnel vision world – reminding me of when I used to wear a parker hood as a kid.

'Switch off manners control centre.' 'Check'. I farted and started dribbling.

And so it went on, the further I ascended the more the superfluous bodily functions were switched off, until there was only one overriding command remaining: don't get off your bike before JK.

Back in England, prior to setting off for the Great Divide, a cycling acquaintance had asked me what I was doing it on.

'An Airborne Corsair,' was my reply, and I proceeded to wax lyrical about all of the components I had carefully chosen.

'No, what DRUGS are you doing it on?' he corrected.

I had thought back then that the drug suggestion sounded a bit drastic, and I naively assumed that drugs were only for naughty cyclists who couldn't make the grade. However, if you had asked me on Indiana Pass if I had wanted some Belgium Mix I would no doubt have taken everything that you had. Then again, as I am sure you are now aware, I was clearly a bad cyclist who obviously couldn't the make the grade. Belgium Mix, according to Willy Voet in his book Breaking the Chain, is one of the many ergogenic concoctions that professional cyclists may use, and it includes amphetamines, caffeine, cocaine, heroine, painkillers, and corticosteroids. Indeed, according to Voet, it is every cyclist's dream to be able to ride up a hill comfortably without the pain, and he alleges that it is this, not the drugs, that they are addicted to. Interestingly, it is further alleged that it was a drugs overdose that brought about the premature death of Tom Simpson on Mount Ventoux. In reality I would have probably declined your kind offer of Belgium Mix as it sounds too much like trail mix, and the thought of scoffing the curry flavoured bag of nuts, raisins and M&Ms made me want to puke.

I don't know whether it was lack of forethought, the misguided assumption that we would be fine, downright stupidity, or just wanting to do it clean, but we didn't have an ergogenic substance between us. JK had plundered our Vitamin I stash during his knackered leg period and we hadn't thought to restock it. Even our coffee bags were decaf.

'Have we got any chocolate?' I rasped at JK like a beggar pleading for spare change. I was hoping my body would be able to extort the caffeine from the chocolate and give me a stimulatory crutch to the top.

JK wearily shook his head, 'figs, cheese slices, or water; that's all I've got.'

I had plenty of water in my Camelbak and the thought of figs and cheese made me want to retch.

'I haven't even got any ephedrine,' he hissed, shooting me a sideward glance and spraying me with spittle.

The 'manners' and 'friendly' centres in his brain had obviously been shut down as well. The hay fever tablets I had coerced JK in to taking, as a result of my zero-tolerance sleeping policy, had contained ephedrine. It is an effective over-the-counter drug that is available in capsule, drink and chewing gum form and is used to treat respiratory problems such as hay fever and flu. But it is also up there alongside blood doping, EPO, and steroids as the professional cyclists drug of choice. Ephedrine is extracted from the ephedra plant and has an amphetamine-like affect on the heart and nervous system. It ramps up the user's heart rate and because of the resulting enhanced supply of oxygen to the muscles it enables the rider to exercise at a higher than normal level for long periods of time. Some cyclists even combine it synergistically with caffeine – another readily available stimulant – for maximum effect. I say readily available, but of course we didn't have any. As it was we had to tackle Indiana Pass unaided, an act of self flagellation I am sure Los Hermanos Penitentes would have been proud of.

Without the drugs distracting my central nervous system, I had to deal with my loose cannon brain and stop it from settling on the idea that all of the pain and discomfort would subside if I just stopped pedalling, got off Corsair and lay down. Of course if I had done that the recriminations would have started immediately and JK would have basked in his triumph. It reminded me of my school days when we used to perform the Queens College shuttle run test. It is a fitness test where you have to run between two cones (that are about twenty yards apart) and keep in time with a series of beeps whose frequency increases. The only thing motivating 1C to keep running was the avoidance of being the first person to quit. As soon as someone did, we all pulled out on the next lap with our egos intact. I prayed for JK to dismount – no, even better – to fall off.

The route wound its way up to Summitville, a misnomer if there ever was one. To me Summitville would be the apex of the climb, but oh no not here, indeed the trail notes read: "start *climbing* away from Summitville". More frustratingly there were no services. I busied my mind with the mathematical conundrum of estimating our arrival time at the summit proper but the ensuing mental arithmetic was akin to running up a down escalator. Each time I glanced at the odometer to give me an indication of how far it was to the top, I would also make a note of my speed and calculate how long it would take. I was slowing down the steeper it became, which frustratingly meant that each time I looked, I always had two hours to the summit. Three hours later we topped out.

The summit, as well as being a topographical highpoint, was also a mental and emotional acme. Not surprisingly, it was also a physiological low point. Lying on my back, watching the grey clouds, I became overwhelmed with pride – I had given it my all and had made it to the highest point of the entire route (and what's more I did it without dabbing). For the first time in four weeks I actually felt that we were going to get to Antelope Wells within our schedule; we had done the hardest part of the route, our mettle had been tested and we were up to the job. Roll on Mexico.

'That was piss easy,' JK breathed, after about half an hour of lying prone.

'What was? Oh that little hill,' I nonchalantly replied, 'Christ I didn't even notice it,'

'Indiana Pass, *Schmindiana Pass*,' he shouted, flicking two fingers up at the trail we had just climbed.

We soon learned that the San Juan Mountains don't appreciate such insubordination and within minutes of our disrespectful display a huge roar of thunder heralded the beginning of a raging storm. A rainsquall moved towards us like a dark theatre curtain across a stage. What was I saying earlier about believing in Karma? If only we had left well enough alone; the clouds had been a blessing. We should have just cycled up and cycled down. But oh no we had to take the piss. Well now it was time to take some shit as well. Our next possible sanctuary was twenty five miles down trail, a place called Platoro, which was described in the trail notes as possibly having an operational café (and on the map it had a trolley, a knife and fork, and a bed). For the next twelve miles the trail followed the contour of the mountain which meant we had to stay at about eleven and a half thousand feet for over an hour. Forks of lightening struck out from the boiling clouds and I was increasingly aware that I was riding a metal bicycle on an exposed mountain in an electrical storm. My knowledge of the metallurgic properties of titanium and whether or not it is a good conductor of electricity was sketchy at best, but I didn't want to find out the hard way. The sheet rain began and as I stopped to get my waterproof jacket out of my sausage bag, I was faced with the realisation that I had packed it at the bottom of the bag. Bar pulling all of my clothes out, there was no easy way to access the jacket. Within seconds my entire wardrobe was saturated, including what I was wearing rendering the waterproof useless. But it did prevent the cold wind that was now sweeping across the mountain from sapping the heat from my bones. We were both despondent; we were fatigued, hungry, cold and wet. As was now becoming a familiar cycle, my enthusiasm and mood took a nose dive; my morale plummeted from the recent euphoric state of believing the route was within my capabilities, to wondering if it could possibly get any worse. Then came the timely puncture. Watching me replace the inner tube must have been like watching the opening credits of The Incredible Hulk, the scene were David Banner is changing a wheel on his car in the driving rain and when he attempts to undue the nuts on the axle he slips and injures his hand. With fingers that felt and behaved like frozen sausages I tried again and again to insert a tyre lever under the bead of the tyre and prise it off the wheel rim. Because it was the new rear tyre that I had fitted at Steamboat Springs, the beading was still taut and was being a real obstinate bastard. Several times I lost the purchase on the tyre lever and my hand slipped, causing me to effectively punch the spokes. Several times I heard JK laugh.

Eventually I managed to refit the inner tube, but it wasn't before my body temperature had cooled. In road cycling, climbs have always presented a homeostatic paradox for the riders. On the climbs the heat produced from the exercising muscles quickly accumulates and needs to be dissipated otherwise the rider's performance will suffer. A short sleeve cycling jersey and profuse amounts of sweat are the solution to this. Then within an instant, the rider crests the climb and the metabolic heat is turned off and the sweat soaked clothes that were a great help moments earlier now rob the rider of his body heat. The increased speed effectively produces a wind-chill factor that cools the rider down even further. The obvious answer is to put on more clothing, but the time it takes to do this could be the difference between winning and losing – especially when you consider the inordinate amount of effort a rider may have put in on a climb just to get a couple of seconds lead on his competitors. An old trick was to have a coach pass the competitor a newspaper which he would then stuff down the front of his jersey as a makeshift windproof lining. Reflecting that John Stamstad, my virtual competitor, had effectively finished the race over a week earlier, I decided that wasting a few seconds to put an extra layer on wouldn't have a dramatic effect on my route time. The extra wet clothes didn't do much good and my hands and feet remained painfully cold, and the faster I plummeted downhill the colder I got.

Since the top, things had changed, there was a nasty, hostile ambiance to the place. And as if to underline the mountains unreceptive grudge, we passed by the

Summitville Mine EPA Superfund Site, the associated trail notes read: "creeks running through this area are contaminated." The water for several miles downstream was highly toxic and unsuitable for drinking even after filtering. The contamination is a saddening example of man raping the earth for its precious metals; the mining companies extorted the gold and with a blatant disregard for the environment they allowed the noxious by-products of smelting to leach into the ground and river water killing the surrounding flora and fauna. It looks like we weren't the only ones to fuck with the mountain.

The descent to Platoro proved to be a similar scenario to the ascent, the colder I got the more I applied the brakes and as a result my speed became progressively slower rendering my arrival time as always an hour away. As we meandered our way down the mountainside I was relieved to catch glimpses through the trees of lights and buildings in the valley below. Platoro was now in sight, so I decided to trade being cold for a swift arrival and I released my brakes for the last couple of miles and splashed my frozen way into the small town.

To our delight the main building in town, the Skyline Lodge, was a three in one business venture; it was a mini mercantile, a restaurant and a bed and breakfast. The rain had now reached biblical proportions. We left the bikes outside on the Lodge's veranda and made our way up the steps towards the entrance. The door opened before we got to it and a kind hearted hostess beckoned us inside.

'Sit yourselves down,' she said, pulling up a couple of chairs for us in the vestibule, 'you look like you could do with some coffee to pick you up.'

I wondered momentarily whether 20mg of ephedrine would be out of the question, but I decided not to push my luck. She promptly returned with two large mugs of coffee on a tray.

'I've put plenty of sugar in them for you,' she said in a concerned voice, 'now don't be afraid to help yourself to the rest,' she added and set a pot of coffee on the table next to me. Then she vanished. While we were hunched over our coffees a crowd of locals had gathered in front of us and were studying us like biologists might when presented with a new animal that they have to assign to a species. As the caffeine and sugar kicked in and as my body began to thaw, I became aware of muffled questions from the crowd.

'Shoot! What the hell are you guys doin' out in a storm like that?'

'Have you had any punctures?'

'You're English right? I've got a cousin in London, do you know him?'

I poured myself another coffee and slowly my surroundings galvanised from the surreal to the real and I was able to hold a conversation with the audience. I also had a question of my own:

'Can I see a menu please?'

We were ushered into the dining area of the haven and were presented with a menu that any restaurant on Piccadilly would be proud of. I ordered a soup of the day, trout with boiled potatoes and salad, and a cafetière of full strength coffee. There is nothing like living off the land and indeed this was nothing like living off the land. Some of the locals had followed us into the dining area wanting more tales and as our blood sugar approached life-supporting levels we obliged.

'There's a phase round here that we say to people like you,' one guy commentated, adding 'vaya con dios.'

That was the second time I heard it, the first time was from the construction worker at the road works near Silverthorne.

'What does it mean?' asked JK.

'Fuck with the mountains and they will fuck with you,' I silently answered smiling to myself.

'God be with you,' he answered and shook our hands.

Now it made sense.

A few paces later we were in the mercantile area of the enterprise cradling armfuls of trail fodder. On the menu for the forthcoming days was Nutrigrain bars, tins of baked beans, and dehydrated potatoes. The cabinet that had once housed the mercantile's candy bars was now empty apart from Fig Newtons and trail mix. Warm, fed and with our food caches distended with fresh trail fodder things were now looking up.

'Is it possible to book a twin room?' JK inquired whilst paying for our groceries.

'I don't think we are letting any rooms out yet,' was the casual reply that can only come from someone who has already got a warm bed for the night.

JK and I looked at each other wide-eyed, looked at the rain lashing at the window, looked at each other again and then pleaded with the cashier.

'Anywhere will do,' I begged, 'even just a bit of floor space.'

'We just need a dry night,' JK added.

'I'll see what I can do,' she replied.

It was going to be a fight to the end, the mountain gods weren't going to make life easy for us. We retired to the chairs in the vestibule and helped ourselves to coffee whilst waiting for the verdict. I was feeling infinitely better than the last time I had sat in the chair, but my fate for the night was still in the balance. I must have nodded off at some point because I was woken by an ecstatic JK.

'We're in, we've got a room, and it's got beds and everything!' he said excitedly shaking my shoulder, then disappeared up a flight of stairs clutching all of his gear. I followed groggily. We converted the pristine room into student digs within a matter of minutes; damp clothes and sleeping bags were draped over every piece of furniture and the room took on a musty smell that any Seattle garbage can rummager would be familiar with. With the household chores in hand I went for a shower.

Afterwards, warm, well fed, clean and dry, I lay on my bed and pondered the wise words Martin Buser had once told me several years earlier. Martin is an experienced competitive dogsled musher and he was a guest speaker at the pre-race meeting for the IditaSport bike race that I had signed up for. He told the competitors that it was going to get cold, that we would feel exhausted, that we would feel sorry for ourselves, and that at times we would want to quit. But he also said that if we decided to give up we should wait until the following morning to do so. His reasoning was that sometimes things are so bad you want to quit, but if you give things a little more time a change in fortune often happens. Often just getting a good night's sleep can make all of the difference. Furthermore, if you do give up, the next day when you're surrounded with your creature comforts and the hardships seem so far away, you won't forgive yourself and you'll have to wait another twelve months before you can exorcise that demon. Indeed John Stamstad, who has won the most IditaSport mountain bike races, has his own "upped-ante" philosophy, 'while I can still walk, I'm still in the race.'

Martin's was a fitting approach to the Indiana Pass ordeal, if I ever wanted to get off Corsair and call it a day it was then. But literally three hours later I felt back to normal and dare I say it even happy. I flicked through a copy of the National Geographic that was on my bedside table, inside was a disturbing picture of a grieving Croatian refugee leading a funeral procession in the driving rain to a makeshift grave. He was holding his dead baby nephew who was wrapped in Clingfilm. My hardships that day paled into insignificance.

CHAPTER ELEVEN: PLATORO TO ABIQUIU

'Ignorant of my own ignorance'

I ignored Eddy's shrill calls to get me up, choosing instead to savour as much of my time in my nice warm bed as was possible. After all, I didn't know when I was next going to have the luxury of a duvet. After a short while, at the opposite side of the room, JK began shuffling around and sorting his stuff out. His actions eventually prompted me to get up and I conceded to the day's chores. I had forgotten how unkempt we'd made the room look, it reminded me of a sepia photograph of a Victorian laundry house that hangs on the wall of my local pub. By now my packing was well rehearsed and was as autonomous as everyday dialogue. Within minutes the room was back to its former immaculate condition, that is of course in a visual sense; the heavy smell of Seattle's finest garbage cans still hung in the air and I imagine it would for some time to come.

There was a confident ambience as I munched my way through a scrambled egg on toast breakfast. Only this time it wasn't arrogant confidence. We had taken the Great Divide's best punch and although it had hurt (indeed had hurt like hell) we were still standing. In terms of the distance we had travelled and the remaining time we had left, we were a little behind schedule, but with the highest altitude behind us, in theory things could only get easier. Altitude training is used by endurance athletes as a way of boosting their athletic performance. The thin hypoxic air causes the body to make up for the shortfall in oxygen by producing more red blood cells (the little oxygen transporters in the blood). When the athletes return to sea level they have a greater ability to carry oxygen in their blood and therefore have the potential to perform better. I was trusting that these physiological adaptations had occurred in our bodies and we would be able to pick up the pace for the remainder of the route. Interestingly the hormone the body produces to signal the production of extra red blood cells is called EPO, and according to Willy Voet in Breaking the Chain it is routinely, not to mention illegally, used by professional cyclists as a performance enhancer. EPO is short for erythropoietin and I wish I had known this before buying a shelf's worth of Evening Primrose Oil from my local chemist. Furthermore I wish I had known that Evening Primrose Oil is used to treat PMS, menopause and breast tenderness, that way I could have avoided the "we get them all in here" looks from the chemist and also avoided shelling out for an expensive collection of useless pills.

The morning started off well, indeed so well that we got some free miles under our tyres without even turning the pedals. At Platoro we changed maps, which put us on map five out of a grand total of six. The free miles came from the overlap of maps four and five, and because of this we started the day 8 miles into map five. Since the beginning of the ride, and especially so more recently, Indiana Pass had preoccupied most of my waking thoughts and it was therefore strange to be setting off without the dread of it sitting on my shoulders like a sack of coal. But a goal achieved is goal lost, and so I refocused my thoughts on Antelope Wells, the fabled end of our journey.

The morning air was cold as we cycled out of Platoro following the Conejos River along the valley floor, and ironically there was no climbing for us to generate much in the way of body heat. Through chattering teeth I cursed the flatness and momentarily wished for the sweltering heat of Helena. An hour or so later the sun burst into view as it cleared the tops of the surrounding San Juan Mountains. This spectacular display coincided with our arrival at State Highway 17 and the beginning of a steep climb up to La Manga Pass at 10,230 feet. And oh, how I cursed the heat. I had come to visualise the Great Divide as being an isosceles triangle whose wide base stretched from Roosville to Antelope Wells and whose apex was Indiana Pass. I felt slightly aggrieved that I should be climbing again, but as ever it was just a case of getting on with it. At the summit we had a quick map check. 'La Manga Pass, elevation 10,230 feet' read the map, 'Nice camping over the next few rolling miles'. If only.

After a switchback descent we turned off the highway and back onto the corrugated dirt. In doing so we crossed the narrow gauge tracks of the Cumbres and Toltec Scenic Railroad. The tracks were first laid in 1880 as a vital link for the Denver and Rio Grande Railroad to the silver-rich mines of southwestern Colorado. It follows that when the silver mining died out so too did the railway, however with geeks being the internationally resourceful and determined bunch that they are, the line was restored and reopened as a tourist attraction in the early 1970s. For any nerds amongst you, here's a little trivia gem: the Cumbres and Toltec Scenic Railroad is both the longest and highest narrow-gauge railway in the United States of America. Wow!

'If you're lucky, or a particularly good planner, you might time your crossing to coincide with the passing of the train,' noted a little sidebar on the map. Unsurprisingly, as we are both unlucky and hopeless planners, our crossing coincided with nothing more than passing tumbleweed.

We left the Rio Grande National Forest to a rendition of our spurious *'Her name is Rio and she dances on the sand...'* lyrics and simultaneously entered the Carson National

Forest with an encore because we couldn't think of a suitable alternative soundtrack. In doing so we also left Colorado behind and entered New Mexico the final state on the Great Divide before Mexico itself.

The scenery in New Mexico didn't change much. I don't know why I expected it to, after all the division was only a state line, and as the trail arced in an annoying easterly direction, skirting the Cruces Basin Wilderness, we were treated to some of the best landscapes of the Great Divide so far. Writing for Airborne.net John Stamstad succinctly reviewed New Mexico as 'horribly primitive roads, brutal climbing, very few services... It was also the most beautiful.' Well I agree with him with regard to the roads, the services, and the beauty, but we hadn't encountered any brutal climbs since crossing the border. Hang on, I stand corrected. Brazos Ridge only gets a passing mention in the trail notes, but it calls for more than that. A lot more. It warrants the likes of John Stamstad, not JK or myself. The climb up to the ridge was ferociously steep and I was caught in a conundrum as to the best riding position; if I adopted my normal riding stance the grade meant that Corsair's front wheel would unweight and bob around with a will of its own. If I leant forward in order to prevent this from happening then the rear wheel would unweight and wash out on every pedal stroke. Annoyingly the climb was strewn with rocks the size of babies' heads, and because my front wheel was obscured by my bar bag I couldn't avoid them. To make matters worse one of the lenses on my sunglasses had steamed up, unfortunately it wasn't the same eye that had sweat dripping into it, thus I was rendered half blind and with no depth of vision. The ascent took us back up into the thin air and because I was constantly changing my riding position I was using more muscles and requiring more oxygen – just as the oxygen was becoming less available. Unbeknown to most anthropologists and physiologists, there exists a primeval human survival function in response to hypoxia that I discovered that morning. At first I thought it was a bear. Then I realised that it was a distressed cow trying to bark like a dog. Then to my astonishment I realised I was making these inhuman yowls. Bizarrely the noise was produced when I forcefully inhaled air, rather than exhaled, and was in a similar manner to a guppy stranded on a river bank. The gulped inhalations were forceful enough to burst open my chest strap on my *Camelbak*, but they proved useful enough to stop me from fainting. Suddenly, aiming to arrive at Antelope Wells was far too distant a goal; in order to survive this climb with my ego intact (JK hadn't dismounted yet) I had to think more on the micro level - just get me to the next bend in the switchback. Invariably each time I got to that mini goal I was greeted with

120

more babies' heads winding their way up to another switchback. Please excuse me while I bark.

Without a doubt Brazos Ridge was harder than Indiana Pass. Maybe the difficulty was only perceived because I had let my guard down after tackling the biggy. Either way, I don't recall the feeling of asphyxiation and nausea being as intense on Indiana. Inevitably the gradient lessened until it flattened out at the summit. I leant Corsair against a tree and sprawled out on my back in the middle of a pretty meadow. I lay there gulping at the air as if each one was my last breath, and it was at least twenty minutes before my respiration returned to anything that resembled normal. I couldn't work it out why I just didn't get off and push. It wasn't as if pushing would have been any slower, indeed it would have been a lot more economical. I hadn't ever felt that much discomfort before, and what is nonsensical is that it was all self-inflicted, or more accurately it was governed by my ego. Rather than have JK beat me, I put myself through a staggering amount of distress, yet the irony was that he was doing the same. How futile, if only we had come to some sort of arrangement that we wouldn't take the moral high ground then all of the stress could have been avoided. As a child I had a friend who was caught up in a similar scenario. He used to get up at an ungodly hour to be driven miles by his doting parents to swimming lessons three times a week. Initially he had begged his parents to take him, but as more interesting things came along (read: girls) he constantly moaned to me that he wanted to quit the swimming, but didn't want to let his folks down. His parents continually offered him support and eagerly gave him a lift each morning yet, unbeknown to us at the time, they were commenting to my parents that they wished he would get fed up with the swimming because they found all of the toing-and-froing a hassle but didn't want to let their son down.

Of course in reality, if JK had sensibly approached me with the suggestion that we walked our bicycles I would probably have milked it for all its worth and played the childish 'well if you think it is too difficult for *you*, I will push with you if it will help' card.

Eventually I unsteadily scrambled to my feet and remounted Corsair. I shakily continued along Brazos Ridge whilst my body attempted to come to terms with the earlier trauma that it had put itself through. We stopped cycling at a signpost that read 'Brazos Ridge Overlook', but it was no good, even the beautiful views of Cruces Basin Wilderness couldn't put the get-up-and-go back into my legs. Instead I got-off-and-lay-down. We were only about fifty miles into the day's ride and in theory, being south of Indiana Pass we should have been putting in triple figure distances with ease. Once again, I was staggered by how genuine professional cyclists are able to ride over a hundred and fifty miles in a day, and then do the same day after day. With these phenomenal feats as a backdrop, I was feeling a little disappointed with myself and I couldn't decide whether I had pushed my body to its limit or whether the physical symptoms were just manifestations of mental fatigue. Todd Balf's feature on John Stamstad in Outside magazine may hold the secret to Stamstad's relentless determination, 'I just make the decision that I'm going to finish, no matter what' says Stamstad, 'that way, I never have to decide whether to quit, because its just not an option. If you go into a race saying, "if I get really tired, I'll just drop out," no matter how mentally strong you are, you'll take the easy way out.'

I don't think I had the mental determination not to quit, but fortunately my surroundings didn't give me the option. Apart from staying where I was and withering away, the only sensible thing to do was to continue. And so we did.

The topography of Brazos Ridge was represented by a wavy line on the map and if you consider that a flat profile generally represents undulating terrain, then I'm sure you can imagine the roller coaster trails we had to negotiate. To make matters worse there was an incessant headwind that could rival anything Montana had thrown at us. I hate the wind. I don't mind cycling in the rain or snow because you can dress accordingly, but the wind – its as though you are cycling as hard as you can and a giant has his hand on your forehead gently pushing you backwards. Eventually the trail bore downhill and we got some respite from the rollers and the wind as we rode down through some spectacular aspen groves. We passed a sign informing us that we had entered Cisneros Park, and as we did so the southern Colorado Mountains were visible to the west, and even better, immediately east a primitive campsite came into view. Without needing to communicate, we silently dismounted and set up camp in this staggeringly beautiful wilderness.

Over our evening meal the conversation turned to how long it was going to take before we reached Antelope Wells. That day we had ridden just under eighty miles, making an odometer total of 1832. This meant that we still had 638 miles remaining and using that day's total as an average it meant we had a further eight days on the trail, giving us an extrapolated tally of 37 days to ride the Great Divide end to end. That put us just outside double John Stamstad's record ride of 18 days 5 hours giving my spurious 'I'm half as good as any athlete' theory a shot in the arm, which I am still not sure is a good thing or not. As you have probably realised it doesn't take much to re-ignite the professional cyclist dream within me, and I immediately set about a rudimentary stretching routine and spouted off to JK about the virtues of being well-hydrated and the importance of eating a high carbohydrate diet. Once again I had my ignorance filter set to high, as I chose to overlook the startling fact that John Stamstad could in theory ride from Roosville to Antelope Wells and back in the time it took me to ride the Great Divide in one direction. Ignorant of my own ignorance, I fell sound asleep as soon as I got into my sleeping bag.

***

At about 3.00 am I had to leave the relative comfort of my slumber and answer the call of nature. Standing there alone in the dark wilderness, I was memorised by the seemingly orchestrated sounds of unseen animals and insects. Every so often the melody was punctuated with a heavy bass footstep that could only belong to a large mammal. Fortunately it was dark so I couldn't see the perpetrator, and I was glad when my urination had finally finished. Returning to the tent, I was appalled by the abhorrent smell of our living quarters. The Seattle garbage-can smell was back with a vengeance. I suppose 'back' suggests that it had left at some time or other. This is not true, it was omnipresent, only at times it was in the background, but now it was obtrusively in the foreground. I queasily settled back into my sleeping bag and took short breaths until the nausea diminished.

'I think we've got a hygiene problem,' I mentioned to JK over breakfast, 'we need to get to a motel and clean ourselves up.'

'I know what you mean,' he replied, 'all of my clothes have taken on an unwashed waxy feel,' he added, holding up a pair of cycling shorts to illustrate his point; they were adorned with dried sweat-salt chromatography patterns. I looked down at my own cycling jersey which had taken on the appearance of a '80s tie-dye T-shirt, only the dye was remnants of food and Gatorade that I had tried to consume whilst riding, unevenly mixed with sweat. Fortuitously our destination for the evening was the 'full services' Abiquiu where we could have a thorough clean up.

The trail continued pretty much as we had left it the previous evening. We meandered along mountainous highland trails and if it were not for having seen the New Mexico state sign, I would have thought we were still in Colorado. The high level riding and soaring morning temperature meant that surface water was difficult to find (no, make that non-existent). So much for my recommendations about being well-hydrated. Once again I met resistance as I sucked on my Camalbak tube, abruptly indicating that I had run out of water.

'Have you got any spare water, mate?' I asked JK, extending an arm to receive one of his handlebar mounted bidons.

'No, I'm all out. Have been for a few miles.'

It's sobering how in the most dangerous places, such as the Great Divide Basin desert, we meticulously planned our water caches and therefore rendered the environment less hazardous, yet in a far less risky area our laisser faire approach caused it to be potentially lethal.

Maybe it was a placebo effect, but I soon began feeling dehydrated. Apparently it only takes a loss of 1% of your bodyweight as sweat to adversely affect your physical performance by 2%. And what's more if you're thirsty you've already lost 1%. As the sweat dripped down off my nose and onto Corsair's top tube I was acutely aware that I was losing fluid from my now finite stores. This was as good as it was going to get unless we were to discover some surface water. We plodded along the corrugated roller coaster dirt tracks with the sun bearing down on us. Eventually we reached Federal Highway 64, and had a map reference stop. The road wiggled its way west and then disappeared under the map legend that displayed the route's profile, thus obscuring any villages that might be a potential water source. The bit of road that wiggled east did so for a couple of inches before disappearing off the edge of the map. However there was a bit of optimism in the form of Hopewell Lake about five miles west. With no other option we headed in that direction.

One of the problems with not having any water is that not only can you not drink, but you cannot eat either. We had been forced to skip a couple of our mandatory hourly food breaks because we didn't have any water to help wash the food down. I started to get the now familiar tunnel vision and weakness feelings that I had come to associate with hitting the wall. I was eyeing up the packet of Ritz crackers sticking out of the mesh pockets on my bar bag in the same way the Wiley Coyote eyes up Roadrunner. And with the same futility as the hapless canine, I knew there was no possibility that I could eat my quarry. We snaked our way up the blacktop which was radiating heat in overwhelming waves. My heart was labouring having to pump my slurry-like blood to my working muscles, and the increase in viscosity meant I could feel every beat as it was pumped through the vessels in my temples. My peripheral vision began clouding over and on several occasions I had to make an emergency swerve in order to prevent myself from toppling over. I strained to fix my waning concentration on JK's rear wheel, and in doing so I hypnotically forgot about my pitiful predicament. I snapped out of my trance when JK's tyre stopped rotating and the tread pattern abruptly came into focus. I unclipped my shoes from the Corsair's pedals and stood astride the top tube with my head on my bar bag. I was aware of my laboured breathing and my swimming head; I felt sick and thought I was going to faint. But we were at Hopewell Lake, and with a name like that I should be rehydrated and feeling back to normal in next to no time.

'Fucking great,' said JK in a tone that suggested he was being sarcastic.

I woozily raised my head to see JK standing by a manually operated water pump. 'What's up?' I inquired.

'Fucking Hopewell, more like *fucking-no-well*,' JK hissed, 'there's no fucking handle on the pump.'

Slowly my surroundings began to make sense. We were in a picnic and camping area and the lake was still a few hundred yards up a dirt track. Resigned I clipped back into Corsair's pedals and followed JK's tyre to the water's edge.

'We're running a bit low on iodine tabs,' JK said rattling the small tablet bottle and holding it up in the light, 'suppose we'd better filter the water and keep the iodine back in reserve.'

I unzipped the frame bag that hung under Corsair's top tube and tossed the water filter to JK. He headed down to the edge of the lake and began pumping. I suddenly realised that I had broken it back at Beaver Dam campground. I was just about to tell JK when he shouted back, 'shit, I've broken the water filter.'

'Oh great, that's just what we need,' I reacted letting myself off the hook, but there was also an uncharacteristic venom in my voice which I immediately regretted.

'Sorry mate,' JK apologised, 'looks like we'll have to use the tabs after all,' he said calmly.

It was infuriating and I guess humbling, that JK was so agreeable when I was in such a bitch of a mood. That said it does seem to work the other way around as well, and this is where I would envisage problems if I was attempting the ride solo à la John Stamstad. At least when there's two of you the chances of you both being on a downer at the same time aren't that high, and the one who is in good spirits tends to pull the other one through the gloom.

We filled our Camalbak bladders and bidons with the lake water and as I held the transparent bladders up to the light they reminded me of the jam jars containing river specimens we used to have lined up on shelves in my old biology classroom. The murky bladder water visibly contained traces of plant, silt and microorganisms. It was soon to contain a good dose of iodine, but I suppose even the best filters and most potent iodine wouldn't be able to remove any of the radioactive waste that had probably leached its way into the lake. These thoughts are post ride reflections, at the time it was all I could do to stop myself guzzling the water straight from the source. Annoyingly the iodine takes about twenty minutes to have its full cleansing effect. I decided to gave it fifteen figuring that my fully fledged garbage gut could fend off a bit of giardia with its hands tied behind its back. My head was now in quite a lot of pain. If you can image a strip of leather tied around your head, and then someone inserting a piece of dowel underneath it and turning it so that the leather strap constricts. Well my head felt like a few turns had already been put in and that on the next turn either the leather was going to snap or by head was going to implode.

After the fifteen minute watershed I sucked on the Camalbak valve with all of the desperation of a runt piglet finally finding a free teat. For five solid minutes I sucked back on the fetid water, pausing only to draw breath. My captor let go of the dowel and as it unwound the leather strap's grip lessened, and the headache receded. With my lucidity came the realisation that another climb was imminent. 'You'll find yourself riding either uphill or downhill but rarely on the level,' read the trail notes in a matter-of-fact way, and with far less sympathy than I cared for. If it was anyone's fault that there still remained a lot of climbing to be done it was the Pleistocene glaciers that sculptured the Tusas mountains many millennia ago. They were long since gone and I'm sure that they wouldn't have cared one iota at our bleating protestations. We put in an arduous 1500 foot climb to the summit of Burned Mountain and I was feeling somewhat burned out myself. We picked up a little road and coasted downhill admiring the stunning views of a beautiful open basin and it wasn't long before we entered the endearing farming village Cañon Plaza. The area has a rich history dating back to the 1770s and the Spanish colonial days. The Spanish influence is still present to this day and so too is an entrepreneurial spirit, which in this instance took the angelical form of a Snack Stand. The trail notes had mentioned that it might be open, but that didn't give us much confidence especially when you consider that other facilities that are mentioned in the notes often don't exist. But our luck was in and the Snack Stand was ready for business. Little more than a wooden shed packed with junk food and a microwave it would easily be passed by preoccupied motorists. To us it was a shrine to the all-important Calorie, and it was time to worship. We dumped our bikes at the front of the stand and shouted for assistance. Our pleas were answered by the firing up of an ATV outside the house on the edge of whose garden the Snack Stand resided. A teenage Hispanic boy dressed in basketball clothing drove to meet us. 'Hi,' he beamed, and his eager little brother skidded to a halt next to him on his oversized mountain bike. The basketball kid unlocked the stable doors of the stand and placed a couple of plastic patio chairs outside on the roadside. Inside the stand, America's favourite junk food was arranged in neat piles. I tucked a tube of Pringles under each arm for starters and then began looking proper. Soft dough chocolate chip cookies, blue Gatorade, rice cakes, and yes! ...a tin of pilchards.

We sat outside in the afternoon sun and ate our collage of food. The basketball kid was sporting a shaven head with a thin rat tail at the back. He was in his mid-teens but had a maturity that was beyond his years. He asked us about our life on trail and offered some advice about the weather and the terrain in the immediate vicinity. He was running the Snack Stand for his parents and he gets a cut of the day's takings for his troubles. Business has been a bit slow of late, but he was philosophical about it, 'I don't earn as much, but at least I can play more basketball.'

Fair enough.

His shy younger brother whispered in his ear.

'He says he would like to show how good he is at wheelies,' the basketball kid said in a tone that suggested we shouldn't expect anything too spectacular.

'Cool, let's see,' I enthused.

He eagerly jumped on his outsized mountain bike and rode up the road for about fifty yards. He then turned around and started riding back towards as fast as he could. As soon as he reached his terminal velocity he stood up on the pedals and jerked the front wheel off the ground a couple of inches, and then as the front wheel touched down he lost control and rode straight into the side of the stand. Instinctively he picked his crumpled body up and tried to get back on his bike, but the handlebars had twisted through ninety degrees making it impossible to ride. His brother was now laughing heartily at him, and in a fit of embarrassment and no doubt considerable pain, the little kid abandoned his bike. Crying into his hands, he ran off towards the house at the other end of the garden. This was our cue to leave.

Refuelled, we bid good day to the basketball kid and headed off along County Road 42 towards Vallecitos. To my astonishment the roadside was just one long rubbish tip. In addition to the ubiquitous porn mags and cassette tape bunting flailing in the wind there was mile upon mile of discarded beer cans and bottles. There were no parking places so the litter was not the result of an alfresco party, rather they must have been thrown from passing vehicles. With the current anti-drink drive culture in Britain I couldn't imagine seeing such a sight on the roadsides back home. Of course I am only referring to beer receptacles and not rubbish; there are plenty of wankers who don't think twice about turning our small island into a tip. The anti-drink drive philosophy seems to be in the minority as I can still remember my astonishment (or perhaps it was delight) when travelling in Australia and discovering that some of the petrol station outlets at the road side were in fact drive through off-licences.

It dawned on me that our present situation was doubly worrying; if we weren't run over by a drunk driver, then we might get hit by an errant bottle or beer can. However these concerns soon vanished into the ether when a couple of ferocious looking dogs appeared out of nowhere and looked like they wanted to pick a fight. We had just entered the hellhole that is Vallecitos. We were skirting a rundown property and fortunately there was a wire fence between us and the slavering canines. As we cycled along the dirt track they were running parallel to us with worrying athletic ease. Shielded by the fence and no doubt buoyed by his recent adrenaline infusion JK made wailing cat noises, and flicking two fingers up at the dogs he commented, 'I think these are yours.'
'Shit!' I shouted and nodded further up the trail.
After about fifty yards the fence ran out, leaving nothing between us and these purpose bred eating machines. Simultaneously we flicked through the gears and stood hard on the pedals. Sensing the start of the action the dogs lengthened their stride, yet still looked as though they had plenty in reserve. There were ten yards to go before the end of the fence. Nine. Eight. We sprinted past a Deliverance extra who was tending a car that had long since died, he straightened himself up folded his arms and seemed content to watch the floor show. He hollered to his son/cousin/wife/brother to come and watch. Five. Four. Three. Two. One. GO! The larger of the two dogs was the first to break free. Out of the corner of my eye I could see him on my left hand side a few feet behind my vulnerable calf muscle. I couldn't afford to look around, but I could hear his close proximity. JK was now a few feet ahead of me and I could see his assailant sticking to him like an Exocet missile, and making periodic snaps at his ankle. Flooded with adrenaline I pushed on with more intensity than I ever could have of my own volition. Then without warning JK's dog stopped, took a snap at me as I passed, but didn't continue with the chase.
'John, It's okay they've stopped,' gasped JK as he slowly pedalled in a hunched position. I turned around to see that my dog had also stopped at the invisible boundary, and I immediately dropped my pace. The dogs trotted back to their Deliverance extra owner, who seemed proud of his lads' performances.
'Fucking freak,' JK muttered between breaths.

After about sixteen miles heading in a general downhill direction we encountered the more attractive and larger town El Rito. El Rito is much a younger settlement than Cañon Plaza or Vallecitos and had slowly evolved from the merging of the original Spanish ranches and haciendas that lined the El Rito River. The day's trip total was getting close to seventy miles and for a moment, as we sipped coffee in El Rito's café, we thought about resting up there for the night. But there were still plenty of hours left in the day, and our legs were feeling pretty strong. And Abiquiu, which had full services status, lay just seventeen paved miles south on State Highway 554. The map profile continued in a downhill direction with only a short, steep climb up to Abiquiu. The journey was entirely on black top and we estimated we should be nicely holed up in a motel within an hour.

At the midway point between El Rito and Abiquiu, the giant ever so gently pressed his hand against my forehead and increased his resistance the more I struggled. The headwind had appeared from nowhere and had reduced our pace to a pedestrian six miles per hour. I was glad of the rest when I punctured. But I was pissed off when I punctured a second time barely two hundred yards further down the road. Worryingly it was in the same wheel; we had done several hundred miles without a puncture and then to get two in the same wheel minutes apart is pushing coincidence a bit. I swapped inner tubes and as we continued cycling I busied my mind with the probabilities of frequent punctures. My thoughts were interrupted by raging complaints from my muscles that they were filling up with the debilitating toxin, lactic acid. I cursed and shouted into the wind, but it was met with a stony silence. I passed the message on to my muscles.

JK broke the agonising silence, 'I think that was Abiquiu,' he said looking back over his shoulder.

'Can't be, the map shows a steep climb before we get to the town,' I said quizzically.

'No, I'm pretty sure that was it,' countered JK, who is rarely wrong about these things.

We turned the bikes round and retraced our tyre tracks. Yep, it was Abiquiu, or more accurately you could call it a mercantile. To give it a full services star was pushing it a bit (no, it was a downright lie). Nonetheless a mercantile is a mercantile and that meant food. We restocked our trail food cache, topped off our water supplies, and abused the restroom facilities. JK inquired as to whether there were any motels in the area, and apparently there was, a mile back up the road was an Inn. We retraced our tyre tracks, but not before a double helping of coffee and donuts.

The celebrated artist Georgia O'Keefe adopted Abiquiu as her home, and I could kind of see why; there was a hippy-magical ambience to the place. For some reason

129

Abiquiu is regarded by certain types as a principal centre of power. For many years it has been a gathering place for the mystically, spiritually, artistically and magically orientated. Folklore has it that witches and wizards used to practise their magic in Abiquiu and it was taken so seriously that in the 1700s that Spanish soldiers were dispatched to cleanse the area of witchcraft. Being branded a witch in Abiquiu in the eighteenth century was not as bad as being convicted of the heinous crime in England. In my local churchyard is a grave of a witch who, after ending her days in the stocks, was buried upside down and a rock placed over her to stop her from escaping. The ritual of spitting on her grave continues to this day. Instead the Abiquiu witches and wizards were only sentenced to serve as house servants for important Spanish colonisers.

The Inn was an impressive adobe building which gave the impression that the tariff was going to be expensive. We hadn't motel'd it for a while so our budget could handle a bit of a dent, but more importantly we needed a wash and our clothes needed de-waxing. The receptionist visibly recoiled as I approached the desk. She looked momentarily embarrassed that she had screwed up her face in reaction to the acrid smell. Then her face turned to stone, 'there are no vacancies,' she said sternly.

The reception was decorated with Georgia O'Keefe paintings and new age type tat. It was also full off meandering well-to-do ladies in their twilight years trying to undergo some kind of belated artistic enlightenment. They smiled genteelly at us, but gave us a wide berth. I couldn't really blame them, after all I was keeping JK at arm's length.

'There is a campsite about seven miles further on,' the receptionist added pointing vaguely over her shoulder. She was painting a very transparent veneer over her overwhelming desire to rid the reception of us god-awful trailhounds.

JK persisted,

'I noticed an RV parked up outside, can we camp there as well?' he inquired leaning on the desk.

'Well, I suppose you can,' she replied recoiling, 'there aren't any facilities, and I'll have to charge you twenty dollars.'

Unperturbed JK paid, and nonchalantly added, 'I take it the restaurant is through here,' gesturing towards the clanking of cutlery. Without waiting for a reply he sauntered off in his proposed direction. I smiled at the receptionist who looked back with a horrified expression, bid her good evening, and with all of the dignity a person dressed in soiled Lycra and cycle shoes can muster, I made my entrance into the restaurant.

The food was most excellent and once again I was able to more than satiate my craving for seafood. We finished off the meal with a double helping of ice cream and coffee. Whilst making the most of the refill policy, we took it in turn to visit the restroom and attempted to clean ourselves up. Timing in these situations is the key and I still hadn't managed to master it. Whilst JK was performing his ablutions, no one in the restaurant needed to use the facilities. However, just when I had stripped down to my shorts and was scrubbing my foot over the hand basin the door opened and a respectable looking gentleman entered. Without breaking stride he used the urinal, and detecting that I was English he engaged me in conversation about the extortionate UK fuel prices. He then bid me a good evening and went about his business as if there was nothing unusual about our encounter. I swapped over feet and the door opened again, this time it was a gentleman who was clearly stunned by what he saw. His eyes widened as I pulled a sheet of dead skin from the sole of my foot and threw it in the waste paper bin, I smiled at him and he turned and made a swift exit.

We settled the bill and I left a good tip for the waitress who had treated us as she would any other guests. Despite our best procrastination efforts, we couldn't delay the inevitable; solemnly we made our way outside and headed towards the tent where we got in our fetid sleeping bags and zipped ourselves into the squalid dome.

'We definitely need to get to a motel tomorrow, 'JK said, then turned over, farted and fell asleep.

'You're not wrong,' I gasped.

'we began playing catch up'

The morning wasn't pretty. Well our surroundings were, but putting on the daily dose of nappy rash cream and pulling on my waxy, acrid shorts certainly wasn't. My socks had taken on a crisp-bag like texture, and my cycling jersey was damp and putrid. I almost passed out when I put my bandana on and inhaled the ammonia of a week's worth of distilled sweat. It had gone beyond the cosmetic; things were beginning to itch.

'Jesus, you've got girl's arms covered with pensioner skin,' JK laughed as I scratched an obstinate itch on my arm.

He was right, my skin had become waxy and flaky and had lost its elasticity. If I pinched my skin between my finger and thumb the ruck of flesh stayed there and didn't recoil. Furthermore my muscles had atrophied, and the once tight sleeves of my Lycra cycle jersey now flapped in the breeze. We were consuming about seven thousand calories a day – almost four times the recommended daily amount – and we were losing weight. Somehow I don't think the Great Divide Diet Plan will ever catch on. Despite JK's mocking he had no right to claim the moral high ground; his once black cycle shorts had now turned a whitish grey due to baked in sweat salt. The sole of his left foot was falling apart, he too had pensioner's skin and his tired eyes were little more than slits. As an antonymic personification of health, we set off down the trail, once again promising ourselves that we would end the night in a motel.

Although the climb up to Abiquiu hadn't materialised yesterday, the climb did exist. The cartographers had been a little premature and the ascent didn't rear its ugly head until we had left town (of course we didn't leave Abiquiu without popping into the mercantile and having our habitual pastry and coffee breakfast). These early morning breakfasts had taken on the designation *Breakfast A*. As a rule we would only have *Breakfast B* when we had cycled our first ten miles, and *Breakfast C* usually coincided with elevenses. Because the terrain was initially tolerable, we were lulled into a false sense of security all of the way to Breakfast B. But trouble was on the horizon, or more accurately the 9367-foot Cerro Pelon Mountain was. With the two Breakfast B Snickers barely in my stomach we began climbing into the Santa Fe National Forest, winding our way up the volcanic ramp of Polvadera Mesa. Because we had been preoccupied with Indiana Pass, we hadn't really checked out the terrain to the south. I generally knew that the maps returned to their green colour rather than the high altitude purple, but that was about it. After all I still had the impression that I was going to be freewheeling along the down slope of the isosceles triangle all of the way to Mexico. Lamentably I was wrong; Polvadera Mesa was a fifteen mile, 4500 foot bitch of a climb. Initially shocked by the incline we stopped for a map reference and instead of knowing what was in wait for us we began playing catch-up with the trail notes and map profiles.

'It says here that it's been called the toughest climb of the entire route,' said JK apathetically reading from the trail notes with his index finger.

And sure enough there in black and white, or rather purple and white, the map profile showed Polvadera Mesa abruptly rising like a graphical representation of a professional footballer's quarterly interest. In a panic I belatedly traced the terrain south of the Mesa, and to my relief it dropped off in a similar fashion to my own bank balance.

Claiming the title of the "toughest climb of the entire route" is no mean feat especially when you're in the neighbourhood of Indiana Pass, but it turned out to be a legitimate call. From the foot of the climb I desperately fumbled for Corsair's lowest gear, something I don't generally like to do. At the beginning of a climb I like to have a few lower gears in reserve so that I can make the going a bit easier if I need to, it's a psychological thing. But Polvadera Mesa had already won the mental battle; I was starting off easy and knew that the next lowest gear was getting off and walking, no doubt quickly followed by lying down. I decided to Amtrak this climb, and for four hours I desperately whirred Corsair's cranks around like a hamster frenetically running around its exercise wheel. After a couple of hours of hamster impressions under the glare of the midday sun we eventually ran out of water. There were no obvious creeks from which we could fill up our Camalbaks and it was looking like we would have to use some valuable time and effort searching off route for the elusive water.

Despite our experiences to the contrary, sometimes the trail gods do give weary trailhounds a break, just when we had decided that we had to go off-trail in search of water we turned around a hairpin to be confronted with our solution. Bernard was a bear of a man who was working in the forests with his buddy installing irrigation systems. His size and gruff beard belied his friendly and helpful nature. He was a lover of the outdoors and had found himself the perfect job; Monday through to Friday Bernard and his co-worker operated the heavy earth moving machinery and camped in the forest. Weekends were spent relaxing with their respective families. Yet apparently you sometimes need to escape from Nirvana.

'Sometimes when this gets too much for me,' he said arcing his hand across the forest, 'I do what you guys are doing, I go and ride my Harley for days on end. Of course I don't have to pedal,' he said laughing.

On the back of his bulldozer Bernard had a huge drum of water and he kindly insisted that we fill up our caches.

'Seriously, you guys are doing some good shit. A man needs to do this sort of thing,' he philosophised stroking his beard.

We chatted for a while, but we could not delay the inevitable. We exchanged well wishes and once gain JK and I pedalled our worldly goods skywards.

Eventually the switchback climbs lessened in gradient and we crested Polvadera Mesa. We had a rest at the top and refuelled our fatigued bodies. The chugging of a laboured combustion engine interrupted the tranquil forest. In a cloud of dust and burned oil and to a fanfare of an un-tuned AM radio, a fatigued Suzuki bubble car skidded to a halt in front of us. How it got up there I have absolutely no idea. Why someone would trust it to get them up there I also have no idea. It was a surreal moment and I knew from past endurance races that hypoglycaemia, lack of sleep and fatigue can cause hallucinations, indeed during the IditaSport race a friend reported seeing the Pope at the trailside handing out chocolate biscuits. I shook my head and blinked hard, but it was still there. I looked across to JK who gave me a confirmatory perplexed look. The dust settled and through the grimy windows I could make out about two Hispanic families crammed into the back of the miniscule car. Two dudes sat up front wearing brightly coloured bandanas and beaming smiles. The driver leant out of his window and bobbing his head, pigeon-style to the noise from the radio asked,

'Hey, is dees de way to Cooba?' and pointed a roll up down the trail in front of the car.

'Yeah, I think so,' I replied, 'according to our map, if you stick to this trail you should end up there.'

It was difficult to hear what he was saying over the radio and the screaming engine noise as he excitedly pumped the accelerator in time with our dialogue.

'You guys look like sheet,' he commented looking me up and down. About four kids faces were now pressed against the quarter light windows watching us gringos. 'Looks like you could do weeth a smoke.'

I thought I heard what he said, but I wasn't sure. I gave him a quizzical look.

'You guys want a joint?' he said slowly, taking a drag on the dirty rollup and then he offered it to me.

I momentarily thought about the pain relief arthritis sufferers purport that marijuana can provide. My aching bones and joints screamed YES! But the last thing I needed was to get high and magnify the munchies that I already had.

'No thanks,' I said shaking my head, 'but maybe later in Cuba,' I added not wanting to offend him.

He offered the joint to JK.

'I'll have some in Cuba,' JK replied.

'You guys are craazee, you don't know what your meesing,' he said and then added 'I'll see you in Cooba, vaya con dios!' And with that he sucked back on the joint, flicked the butt out of the open window, floored the accelerator and the overcrowded jalopy lurched forward at breakneck speed. It then disappeared down the track in a cloud of dust.

'Vaya con dios to you,' I said after them.

Before setting off I had to pump a bit of air into Corsair's rear tyre. I must have picked up a slow puncture somewhere on the climb, but I couldn't be bothered unpacking and repacking the bike for a repair, and I figured that I could probably get away with stopping and inflating it a couple of times before we got to Cuba, our full services destination. There was still thirty odd miles to go, but it was all downhill and should in theory only take two to three hours to get there.

We cruised through the cool hilltop forests and were making good progress; the odd time I had needed to inflate the tyre I had managed to make it coincide with a map reference stop. At about fifteen miles outside of Cuba we were treated to an excellent view of Valle Grande Caldera that was framed by the Jemez Mountains and the distant Sandia and Gila Mountains in the south. The Valle Grande Caldera is a spectacular fourteen mile diameter valley caused by large-scale volcanic action. It was formed about a million years ago when an active volcano in the Jemez Mountains spewed out its molten contents and then, lacking support, imploded. The result of this geographical transformation is enthusiastically described in the trail notes as "one of the most impressive volcanic craters in the world". Although I haven't seen that many, it would certainly take some beating.

The map profiles were fairly accurate this time and the route actually headed downhill. Just as we exited the Santa Fe National Forest Corsair's rear tyre suffered a blowout and we had to stop at the trailside for an emergency repair. I wasn't happy about the sudden increase in punctures I was getting and whilst I had Corsair's rear wheel stripped down I gave it a thorough inspection. The new tyre I had put on back in

135

Steamboat Springs must have been defective; the inner carcass of the tyre was coming apart and rubbing on the inner tube, eventually wearing it away and causing it to puncture. It was pointless refitting the defective tyre as it would eat through our spare inner tube reserve in no time. Fortunately, back in Steamboat Springs I had had an unusual bout of foresight and had zip tied JK's best worn-out tyre to the underside of my saddle. I used this as the replacement tyre, and although it was bald at least it wouldn't devour the inner tube. I planned on getting a new tyre (and a spare one) in Cuba.

With fifteen miles to go to Cuba the forest trail formed a T-junction with State Highway 126. This has got to be the most nebulous use of the word highway ever, I've seen less primitive side roads in Third world countries. It was little more than a dirt track. We swung left and headed sharply downhill. The sun was in its final stages of arcing across the sky, but at this pace we were on schedule to arrive at Cuba before it got dark. It was a good feeling to get some payback for the hard climbing we had put in earlier on in the day. We were flying downhill and I was having a great time dodging the potholes and rocks, it was like an arcade game and demanded total concentration. Then a horrific sight flashed by in my peripheral vision. I anchored on and JK flew past at warp speed.

'John! STOP!' I shouted with my hands cupped around my mouth.

At first I didn't think he had heard me then an enormous plume of dust bellowed out from Vick's rear wheel as JK applied the brakes.

'What is it?' he shouted back.

I beckoned for him to come and look.

'Can you not come down here?' he pleaded, 'I don't want to climb back up.'

'You're going to have to,' I answered.

Resigned, JK started the climb back up to meet me.

'What is it?' he gasped, as he pulled level.

I nodded towards a signpost on my left. JK looked over and visibly deflated as he registered what had happened. The signpost pointed to Cuba, only it was in the direction we had just come down.

'Shit! We should have turned right at the T-junction,' JK muttered, then turned to me and asked, 'how far have we come?'

I looked down at the odometer, 'six miles'.

JK was really pissed off with himself as he had made the call back at the T-junction. We were both tired and it was a simple matter of fatigue affecting our judgement; it was no one's fault, just one of those things. But JK didn't see it like that, he was really cursing himself and apologising for his stupidity. It got so bad that when I suggested that we had

136

a Snickers break he said he didn't deserve one. JK refusing food, things must have been pretty bad in his head. I had second-guessed what his self-inflicted punishment was going to be just before he embarked on it. He was going to attack the climb we had just ridden. I let him go and I finished off my Snickers before clipping in to Corsair's pedals and following him up the climb. A couple of hundred yards in front of me JK was standing out of the saddle pushing a big gear. His demons were getting a thorough exorcising.

We reached the T-junction just as the last of the evening light was beginning to fade. In his anger JK had opened up a considerable gap between us and was hammering really hard. I hoped he would stop at the junction so that we could have a breather but he didn't he just kept going. Now that it was dusk I had a slight vision problem. The sunglasses I was wearing had prescription lenses to correct my myopic eyesight so I needed to wear them to see where I was going, but the dark lenses meant that it was difficult to see anything in the twilight. For some strange reason my normal glasses were in JK's bar bag, which by now was just a speck on the horizon. I moved the sunglasses to the tip of my nose so that I could see through them, or over them if I needed. This was not the ideal solution that I thought it was because I immediately rode Mr Magoo style into a pothole and my glasses flew off into the roadside verge. I then spent ten thoroughly pissed off minutes rummaging around in the roadside amongst the porn mags, cassette tapes and beer bottles before I found them. Honestly I was looking for my glasses.

The primitive track abruptly turned to blacktop and without the fear of hitting another pothole I was able to pocket my sunglasses and pick up the pace. A mile or two up the road I caught up with JK who was resting against a roadside barrier, the backdrop was the twinkling valley of night time Cuba.

'Christ I'm knackered,' JK huffed.

I snorted in agreement. 'You were really hammering it then, it was all I could do to keep you in my sights.'

'I know, I just kept promising myself a deep pan pepperoni pizza with extra cheese if I got us to Cuba.'

At the mere mention of the pizza I was salivating. 'With garlic bread and a huge Coke,' I added.

And with that we silently cruised through the darkness down to Cuba.

Downtown Cuba was a marvellous sight to us two weary trailhounds but I am sure the feeling was not reciprocated by the locals. There were illuminated billboards advertising food, and amongst them was our neon pizza sign. However, before eating we really did need to clean ourselves up, so we pulled up outside a Seven Eleven and asked directions to the cheapest motel. It was easy to find, all we had to do was home in on the thud-thud bass beats of youths in parked cars and the cursing and bottle breaking that tends to accompany this international teenage pastime. The neighbourhood of the Del Prada Motel was not the most salubrious, but the management were courteous and more importantly the room was only twenty dollars.

I headed straight for the shower to perform my ablutions. It took me twenty minutes to scrub and peel off my outer layer of skin, which was made up of a combination of dead skin, dirt, nappy rash cream, sun cream and sweat. The water swirling down the plughole was a filthy brown and I stood under the hot power jet until it ran clean. I then stood there for a further ten minutes; it was the best shower I had ever had. Whilst JK showered I set about cleaning my clothes in the hand basin, and once again I was amazed at how much crap came off them.

With our washing taken care of, we set off up Cuba's main street to satiate our hunger. It was great to be clean and as I walked along in the warm evening air things were feeling good. The closer the pizza sign got the longer our strides became, and we were soon in the pizza aroma zone. As I got to the steps of the restaurant a waitress turned the OPEN sign around and shook her head at me through the glass panelled door. She mouthed, 'we're closed.' I looked up at the neon sign above my head, it flickered twice and went out. Not being able to comprehend the full horror of the situation I glanced across to JK who was shaking his head and looking as if he wanted to break something. It was a cruel, cruel blow.

'I saw a Subway on the way in,' I said looking up the street, and to my horror I saw the Subway sign flicker and die out.

'I thought this was meant to be a twenty-four hour country,' JK muttered to no one in particular.

The once brightly lit street was now looking distinctly non-illuminated. It looked like we would have to pick up more junk food at a gas station and eat it back at the motel. The thought of eating more American candy was not appealing, so much so that if it was going to be our only option I was considering not bothering. However, in our haste to get to the pizzeria we had overlooked a Mexican Restaurant situated next door to the motel. We took a window table and JK ordered an extra large burrito and I opted for two helpings of chicken fajitas. While we were waiting for the food to arrive we wolfed down the complimentary nachos on our table, we also devoured those on the next table and the ones next to that. The chicken lettuce and cheese were delicious and it was the real food that my body had been craving for days.

'It's funny, but on this trip I get emotional just after I've eaten,' JK informed me.

I was only half listening as most of my attention was focused on building my next fajita.

'Well if you want to cry, don't let me stop you,' I half-heartedly replied.

'What are you on about?' JK inquired, 'I said I get a bit of motion not emotion. I'm off for a crap.'

An hour and half earlier I was in a dire state, now as I walked back to the motel things couldn't have been more different. I was clean, fully fed, had some clean clothes for the tomorrow's riding, and the best thing was that I had a real bed for the night. But before getting some much needed sleep we meticulously reviewed the next few days' terrain on the maps, we didn't want another day in the saddle like the one we had just had.

The next morning we had got used to the rich living and decided to have breakfast at the Seven Eleven. The previous day's ride had totalled ninety two miles including the extra twelve we had ridden due to our navigational error. So we decided to take it easy and give our bodies a rest. My clothes washing skills must leave a lot to be desired because as soon had I sat down outside the Seven Eleven with my breakfast two winos approached us and treated us as kindred spirits. Worryingly, apart from the stale urine odour they didn't smell too bad. The first guy asked us for a light.

'Sorry mate, don't smoke,' answered JK.

'Well you light camp fires don't you?' he retorted in a sarcastic tone before staggering off.

The second tramp, who had a resplendent piss stain down the front of his jeans, was more eloquent and struck me as a good bloke who had fallen on hard times. He told us about the days when he was seriously into road cycling, and gave us his opinion on Lance Armstrong's training for the Tour de France that had just finished being waged on the other side of the Atlantic. I told him about my predicament with the bald tyre and asked him whether there was a cyclery in Cuba. In an apologetic manner he confirmed there wasn't, yet helplessly affirmed that if it was up to him there would be one. He also told us that three Alaska women who were also riding the Great Divide had pulled into Cuba the previous morning and so were about a day's worth of riding ahead of us. JK was unusually philosophical about this; his competitive streak would normally have him forgoing his breakfast in favour of overtaking other riders on the trail. Instead he mused,

'I think we should start Breakfast B.'

'Sounds good to me,' I replied, relieved we weren't racing off up the trail.

The town of Cuba began life in the late 1760s and formed part of the San Joaquin del Nacimiento Land Grant given to three dozen Spanish colonizing families. Around a hundred years later it became a ranch community before rapidly developing into the fabled Wild West town that, according to legend, was wild in more ways than one. Even as late as the mid twentieth century Cuba was regarded as a place not to be around after dark. Fortunately for us, Cuba proved to be a pleasant place to stay in overnight, and these days it acts as a more tame service industries town catering for the needs of travellers and truckers rather than gunfighters and desperados.

Breakfast B seamlessly blended into Breakfast C and it wasn't until a couple of hours had passed that we found the impetus to eventually set off along Highway 197. The ride began inauspiciously when a Budweiser bottle that was thrown from a passing pickup narrowly missed my head. I hadn't been wearing my cycling helmet (apart from on the downhills) for the last couple of weeks or so because of the heat, and it was therefore fortuitous that the bottle didn't crack my skull. Lamentably the bottle was empty, so nothing could be salvaged from the incident. I can't say for sure whether it was thrown deliberately but considering there were miles of traffic-free road ahead it seemed beyond coincidence that the driver chose to throw it as he was overtaking us. That initial animosity, rightly or wrongly, put me on edge and made me dislike the area.

The road took us in a south-westerly direction and wound its way through a patchwork of terrain that separates Mesa Chivato and Chaco Mesa. We were bordering on Navajo Indian land but it wasn't reservation land as such, rather it was part of an assortment of lands under various jurisdictions. It looked like we were going to be in this kind of territory for at least two days and because of this it was going to be an issue finding a legal place to set up camp. And the prospect of finding water in this unforgiving barren wasteland wasn't looking too good either.

The sun was out in force and the blacktop was radiating pulses of overwhelming heat. A strong north-westerly wind helped take the edge of the ridiculously high ambient temperature, but although it wasn't head on it was still providing a formidable resistance. Apparently, according to the laws of physics and aerodynamics, only a tailwind that is in a 160 degree segment behind a cyclist will assist the rider in a forward direction. Or put another way there is a 200 degree frontal arc that has the potential to offer resistance. According to the principles of Sod's law this is where today's wind resided. But even the wind wasn't the worst adversary; that job fell to the monotony. As far as I could see the primitive road stretched out into the distance along a series of rollers that bisected a barren, desert-like shrub land. For hours we rode in silence. JK was about one hundred yards ahead of me no doubt doing a tour of his head. I rode along silently watching my shadow's legs pumping up and down on the tarmac next to me. I was thinking about what I was going to do when we finished the ride. At that moment tequila, a large pizza and crate of Budweiser was at the top of my list. I was brought out of my thoughts by the clicking of JK's freewheel. He had moved over to the centre of the road and was coasting waiting for me catch up. He was looking over his right shoulder waiting for me to get into earshot. I nodded to him inquiring what the issue was.

'I've been thinking about finishing the ride,' he said.

I nodded again for him to continue.

'I'm going to commemorate it with a tattoo,' he added.

'Cool. What kind of design?' I asked, glad to have something new to talk and think about.

'Dunno, maybe some kind of Aztec armband, I don't know. But have a think about it,' and with that he pulled forward, and we returned to our repetitive trudge. Glad of a new morsel for my mind to chew on, I spent the next hour or so mentally designing tattoos, my favourite design (and sadly lacking any artistic flare) was a bike chain armband.

After about twenty five miles on State Highway 197 we reached the Navajo settlement Terreon. Here the road became Reservation Road 9 and abruptly swung through ninety degrees taking us in a north-westerly direction. This meant we were riding straight into the oppressive wind; there was no need for a 200 degree buffer zone, this bastard was head on. There's only so much time you can spend thinking about tattoo designs and with a brain that hasn't had anything to think about for weeks a titbit like that doesn't last long. I was glad when a building-like structure appeared on the horizon. It wasn't represented on the map, so we whiled away the time trying to guess what it was going to be. Perhaps a gas station? Or maybe a snack stand? Bizarrely it was a laundrette. For days we had been crying out for one and now when a laundrette with all of the mod cons appears we couldn't afford the time to patronise it. Fortunately, soon after, another building appeared on the horizon which acted as a mental crutch to get us through the next hour. Only this time we knew exactly what it was; according to the map it was a gas station. And I also knew exactly what I wanted: ice cream and blue Gatorade.

Before the gas station there was a Continental Divide crossing, but because we were in the flatlands the climb up to it wasn't noticeable. The gas station proved to be a true oasis; it had a microwave and a kettle for customers to use. We gorged on pies, noodles, Ritz crackers and apples. The attendant told us that the three Alaskan women who were riding the Great Divide had passed through earlier that morning. JK was happy that we were gaining on them and so granted us a second helping of food and an extended break. I bought my ice cream and Gatorade and sat outside in the shade. As I slurped my cookie dough ice cream I read the carton; it proudly displayed a star with the words ARTIFICALLY FLAVOURED emblazoned within it. God alone knows what the chunks of cookie were if they weren't cookies, but they certainly tasted good. The food break didn't last long as JK was keen to get some overtaking done, he knew the Alaskans weren't far away and wanted to overtake them before nightfall. About six miles further up Reservation Road 9 we entered Pueblo Pintado, a small settlement on the edge of Chaco Canyon National Historical Park. The Park is often referred to as the 'Stonehenge of the West' and it was awarded World Heritage status in 1987. Within its boundaries are the ruins of Pueblo Bonito, a five storey building dating back to the ninth century. Apparently it contained about 800 rooms and was inhabited by Native Americans for over three hundred years. I couldn't work out which was the most amazing; the magnitude of the building, or the fact that people lived in such a desolate wilderness for so long.

Propped up outside a building at Pueblo Pintado were three telltale mountain bikes with trailers. We pulled off the road and up a short dusty track to the building. The owners of the bikes were lying prone on a picnic table and were recovering from the incessant headwind they had been cycling into all day. The all female party consisted of a mother, her daughter and a family friend. We stayed and chatted with them for a while, mainly reminiscing about earlier sections of the route which now seemed like a lifetime away. The women had had a tough time on Indiana Pass and had been caught out in a violent storm and had been forced to camp out at the summit. The night spent at altitude had been pretty bad and had taken it out of them. We nodded in agreement, after all we know how vicious Indiana Pass can be if it wants to.

Having got the landowner's permission they were going to camp in the lot outside of the building. It would have been nice to have joined them, but with the "double the world record" target looking very feasible we had to push on. Reservation Road 9 took another abrupt turn out of Pueblo Pintado and generally headed due south. This in theory should have shifted the wind into our favourable 160 degree catchment area, and indeed this would have been the case if the wind hadn't decided to change direction and become a southerly. The afternoon's riding was more of the same; hard cycling against the giant's opposing push. I was becoming increasingly concerned that I hadn't seen anywhere that would have been a good place to camp. There was a wire fence about ten yards either side of the road that intermittently had a sign attached that read PRIVATE LAND NO UNAUTHORISED ACCESS. I didn't relish the idea of camping at the roadside and taking my chances with the drunk drivers and bottle throwers. JK was also anxious about our predicament and we decided that at the next possible place we would stop and make camp. One of the main problems we have encountered when deciding on a place to camp is realising when we've got it good. It is easy to write a potential site off as 'sloping', or 'too may mosquitoes' or whatever because you think that a better one will come along in a mile or so. Only it doesn't and ten miles later your only option is to camp on a forty-five degree slope that is infested with mosquitoes. Of course the reverse has also been true; we have put up with a few annoying idiosyncrasies of a site because we had thought that we wouldn't be able to find a better one, only to find the next morning a perfect site just around the corner. Usually it was a comfort thing, this time I was also concerned about our safety.

Mile after mile nothing presented itself and we passed through the Navajo settlement White Horse as the light was beginning to fade. If all else failed we would have to make camp under the cloak of darkness and rely upon Eddy to get us up at first light. Just outside White Horse the Reservation Road turned into State Highway 509 and about five miles later, near Hospah (another settlement) there was a cluster of trees and bushes at the roadside. We peeled off to the right and stashed Vick and Corsair behind a bush and checked the site out. It was surprisingly ideal; we were sheltered from the road and the ground was relatively flat. This was as good as it was going to get, so we set about erecting our tent and performed our usual setting up camp routine. JK fired up the stove and made a couple of decaf coffees, which we used to wash down our hotchpotch supper that comprised Ritz crackers, Rice Krispie marshmallow cakes and the obligatory Snickers. We sat up chatting as the sun was setting and mulled over the upcoming days. We had just added eighty miles to the odometer and if that kind of daily mileage was to be typical it was looking as if we might have about five days left on the trail. Suddenly, after wanting to get as many miles on the clock as possible, a large part of me was upset that we were nearing the journey's end. After having lived and breathed the Great Divide for so long it seemed strange that it was soon going to be over. The sun finally disappeared over the horizon and as I drained the dregs of my second cup of coffee I watched the headlights of a car as it weaved its way up the road and sped past us with the driver oblivious to our camp. Content we weren't going to be troubled I retired for the night.

CHAPTER THIRTEEN HOSPAH TO WALL LAKE

'the road to opportunity'

Following the long ride into Cuba, yesterday was meant to be an easy day, but by the time we had found somewhere to camp it had become a protracted and tiring one. The idea behind today's ride was to follow the Great Divide route for about fifty miles to a town called Grants. In theory this would give us plenty of time to rest, recover and sort ourselves out for the final push to the finish.

The morning air was chilly, but rather than rush breakfast we donned a few extra clothes and took our time. After having a good night's sleep, and without starting the day with a beer bottle being thrown at me, I looked at my surroundings through different eyes. The first rays of light were making their presence known and they coated the barren land and lava formations with a soft amber glow. Apart from JK slurping his coffee there was nothing to be heard. I reassessed my initial judgement of the area to one that was bowled over by how beautiful the landscape was, reminding me in part of the Great Divide Basin in Wyoming. Thankfully the Wyoming inspired headwind had abated and considering today's ride was entirely on road, we estimated that it wouldn't take us too long to get to Grants. We decided in the interest of self-preservation that we would curtail the pace slightly and enjoy the ride.

About four miles outside a little Indian settlement called Hospah, the Great Divide Route flatly crisscrossed the Continental Divide for a couple of miles. At the beginning of our travels it had taken us five days to get our first Continental Divide crossing under our tyres, but here we had bagged about half a dozen in ten minutes. As we cycled along the northwest flank of the San Mateo Mountains we discussed the supplies we were going to have to procure in Grants in a manner that suggested that riding past piñon studded plateaus and deep arroyos was an everyday occurrence; it was certainly a world away from popping down to my local Asda for groceries. But I suppose that is one of the downsides of spending so long in such beautiful surroundings, it's easy to take them for granted. The unique landscape of this area was the result of a blend of natural and unnatural sculpting forces. The volcanic rock, geography, soil type and weather have created the distinctive topography and the decades of overgrazing by livestock have left the earth barren. The area is also dotted with reminders of the early settlers who tried to eek out a living in this unforgiving land. Ghostly structures made out of rock and other local materials give a tangible hint at how hard life must have been. It was also a reminder of how easy JK and I had it. With only a few days remaining I could see the mod con light at the end of the hardship tunnel, but with another thirty years of adversity stretched out in front of me in order to merely exist, I don't think I would have been able to cope.

Grants, which has a population of around 8,500, was the largest town on the Great Divide that we had visited since Rawlins back in Wyoming. Remarkably the comparison doesn't end there. Where Rawlins marked the end of the parched basin, Grants (according to the trail notes) heralded the end of our current dry spell and abundant surface water was something we were both looking forward to. Grants started life as Los Alamitos which means 'little cottonwoods' back in 1872. The name change occurred just nine years later when three Canadian brothers named Grant developed a train stop there and seeking a bit of recognition they named the town after themselves. They had adroitly secured a contract to build a section of the Atlantic and Pacific Railroad from Isleta Pueblo, New Mexico to Needles, California via Grants and as a result hundreds of workers were brought into the area and the town underwent a boom period. The railway also underwent a name change and was renamed the Santa Fe line, and it was on this line back in 1897 that an armed robbery took place just outside of the town and a reported $100,000 was taken. According to local legend the booty was buried under a nearby juniper tree. Annoyingly these directions are only slightly worse than our maps as there are thousands of juniper trees in the surrounding area, and finding the right one would be like trying to locate a new bike tyre in this town.

The railroad boom didn't last long and the town soon went into recession. But as seems to be the case with most of the towns we've passed through, history shows that it isn't long before another boom comes along. Grants got a second impetus in 1950 when Navejo sheepherder found uranium in the neighbouring Haystack Mountain. It didn't take long for this resource to be exploited and soon thereafter Grants became known as the uranium capital of the world. The town grew exponentially, but since those early heady days the radioactive boom has gone bust, however as a reminder the word uranium cropped up in a few of the street names that we cycled past. Our road joined the historic Route 66 in downtown Grants, and we rode along it to the predictable chorus of '*I get my kicks on Route 66*' and as these were the only lyrics we knew we sang them on a loop. I know it is going to sound hard to believe but it was so bad it made our '*Her name is Rio...*' song sound harmonious.

Route 66 was completed in 1926 and although it was designed for motorised traffic it shares more than a passing resemblance to the Great Divide Mountain Bike

Route. In the days when travelling by car was no mean feat, to traverse the 2400 miles form Chicago to Los Angeles was an adventurous undertaking of epic proportions. In his classic social commentary The Grapes of Wrath John Steinbeck refers to Route 66 as the 'mother road' and that was indeed how it was considered by the travellers of the time. Steinbeck's 1939 novel, which was set during the Great Depression, immortalized Route 66 in the American consciousness. It has been estimated that over 200,000 people migrated to California to escape the desolation of the Dust Bowl. For those who endured the arduous relocation Route 66 symbolized the 'road to opportunity.' Like the Great Divide, Route 66 didn't circumnavigate towns and communities in order to speed up the travelling process; rather it passed through settlements and actually formed the main street of some towns. In a similar manner to riding the Great Divide, travellers were glad to reach civilisation and refresh themselves, and also take time out to admire the spectacular country they were passing through. You won't be surprised to learn that the entrepreneurs were quick to take advantage of the situation; storeowners, motel managers, and gas station attendants recognized early on that even the poorest travellers needed food, car spares and a bed for the night. This resulted in numerous cafes, diners, market stalls, Indian trading posts and other attractions (even snake pits) sprouting up along the roadside.

By all accounts Route 66 was a welcoming highway and it sounds like in its day it would have been a joy to traverse. These days however it is a shell of its former self, and lamentably it proved no match for progress. Ironically, the public lobby for rapid mobility and improved highways that had made Route 66 a success in its formative years also brought about its decline. A leaf was taken out of Hitler's book when General Eisenhower, who had been impressed by the strategic value of Hitler's Autobahn, proposed a road system that allowed Americans to 'drive with speed and safety at the same time.' Progress has taken the form of four lane highways. Back in Route 66's heyday it would have taken a traveller days to traverse the 400 miles across New Mexico from Gallup to Glenrio, whereas nowadays modern motorists can cross the state in a day without having to go through a town. Indeed if they are carrying a full tank of fuel they don't even have to stop. The building of the Interstates did of course spell the demise of the idiosyncratic roadside vendors who have been lost forever and who have been replaced by standardised burger franchises and other outlets owned by petroleum companies.

We patronised one of the former and whilst procuring our caffeine and fat infusion we got the lowdown on the town's other facilities. Across the road was a laundrette and there were three campsites located around the town. We opted for the KOA campsite because the other KOA sites we had used were decent (the irony hadn't escaped us: standardisation, the result of globalisation). Before setting up camp we washed our spare clothes at the laundrette and whilst they were drying we visited the gas station to stock up on food. I was amazed, but not surprised, to learn that Grants didn't have a bicycle shop; this meant that I was going to have to rely on the bald tyre for yet another day. True to form the KOA site was ideal and after having pitched our tent and showered we went in search of additional supplies. Also true to form was the American inability to judge distances correctly.

'How far is it to the nearest supermarket?' I asked the campsite receptionist.

'About two miles,' she answered, 'you can catch a bus from across the street.'

'Thanks, but I think I will walk,' I replied.

She was visibly shocked that humans could walk that far.

As we walked along it was glaringly obvious how everyone was dependant on the automobile; we were the only people who were using Shank's pony. After about half an hour we began to question the receptionist's distance. We were approaching a gas station so we called in to confirm that we were on the right path.

'Yeah, it's about two miles straight up that way,' replied the attendant, pointing in the direction we were heading.

After about three quarters of an hour the supermarket came into view. I suppose the car is to blame for people's lack of ability for judging distances. When you have to put the effort in to cover the ground you develop a thorough knowledge of the relationship between distance and effort. Over the last few weeks I had become very adept at calculating how far we had ridden just by judging how knackered I was as a yardstick. If all you do is press your foot on the gas pedal then I suppose that intimate understanding is lost.

Our two mile journey turned out to be a ten mile round trip, but in the end it wasn't as bad as it sounds as it helped to loosen up my cycle-weary legs. When we got back to the campsite we cooked ourselves a meat and vegetable broth, which for once actually contained real ingredients. As was becoming increasingly commonplace, our mealtime banter turned to finishing the route and we had to start thinking about how we were going to get back to civilisation once we had arrived at Antelope Wells. This was something we hadn't really paid much attention to, and it was looking as though we might have an extra one hundred and forty miles to ride to get to El Paso.

***

Feeling refreshed from yesterday's recovery ride we started day thirty four early with a view to putting in a century ride. There was still over 350 miles to go to the end of our journey and if we were to complete it within double John Stamstad's record time we needed to put in some triple figure miles. We had Breakfast A at the gas station and filled up on trail food. We were starting fully laden with provisions as the next significant town we were scheduled to ride through was Silver City, which was about 250 miles, or about three days worth of riding down the trail. According to our notes once we had left Grants we had also 'left behind most of the high mountain country'. This was good news for my legs, and fortunately it didn't herald the end of the beautiful scenery to which we had become accustomed. Our early morning ride took us into and along the boundary of the El Malpais National Conservation Area. Back at the gas station I had asked what El Malpais meant and a rough translation is 'the badlands.' Thankfully, El Malpais National Conservation Area was not a self-fulfilling prophecy; it is a spectacular, if strange, landscape. The El Malpais National monument resides within the conservation area and is home to several dormant volcanoes that have discharged lava over the surrounding area throughout the millennia. Fortunately the most recent eruption was almost 1000 years ago, but the effects of the volcanoes still dominate the area. According to local Indian folklore there was a time when "fire rock" engulfed and buried their ancestral homelands, and it is widely believed that the tale refers to the most recent eruptions of El Malpais.

We cycled through the bizarre volcanic landscape of hardened lava flows, sandstone bluffs and strange lava-tube caves. Apparently not far from the trail there is an Ice Cave which has, in its innermost bowels, deposits of ice that remain frozen throughout the year despite the outside temperatures soaring (as they were) up to a 100 plus degrees. Unfortunately, even with the temptation of the cooling ice we couldn't deviate from the route (remember: we are professional cyclists, not tourists lest you forget). We filled up our water at a section of the trail called "The Narrows" where there was a basic campsite and after a short break we continued our push south. So far we had been riding on State Highway 117, but shortly after leaving The Narrows we left the El Malpais National Conservation Area and took a direct route south on the usual washboard dirt tracks. In doing so we weaved our way through juniper and piñon forests and across open grasslands. The topography was, as ever, undulating but the hills were more rolling than the usual full-on climbs. Several things inspired me as I rode through the unique New Mexico wilderness; in the southeast I could see the Datil Mountains which I had read about in numerous mountain bike magazines as being an awesome place to ride, in the south were the Sawtooth Mountains and to the southwest I could see Escondido Mountain. But even more inspiring than this chocolate box vista was our next town; it was Pie Town, and you don't get a moniker like that for making crappy pies.

JK was thinking about going for cherry pie with ice cream. Blueberry pie sounded good to me, although the Great Divide grapevine had it on good authority that they also served up a good cheesecake. Before we got there we had to crest the Continental Divide (our eighteenth crossing) and although we were still around 7500 feet above sea level, it was a relatively shallow incline and passed by unnoticed. Our dirt track spewed us out onto Federal Highway 603 and continued straight ahead on the opposite side of the road. But to our left was the fabled pie shop. Although it was off route, and although it was uphill I was prepared to put the effort in, and in an instant I had made my mind up: I was going to have a cherry pie, and a blueberry pie, and a cheesecake. JK was standing hard on his pedals and making a beeline towards the eatery; it looked as though he had also made his mind up.

The town had begun as a result of the mining in this part of New Mexico, and when a forward thinking local businessman with a mining claim in the area learned that Highway 60 was to become a major transcontinental route he opened a diner, and from that moment on the town was set on a course that was going to give it its name. What followed was an extraordinary example of self-promotion. As a result of his road signs advertising the self-proclaimed superiority of his pies, the town gained the nickname Pie Town amongst the travelling fraternity of the time. However the nickname was not enough and eventually the town got the official stamp from the US Postal Service and from then on Pie Town became its formal name.

JK looked back over his shoulder towards me frowning, and my heart sank. 'Please tell me it isn't shut,' I said silently to myself. I eagerly looked at the building for telltale signs of life, but the parking lot at the front was empty and the windows were dark. As we got closer reality hit us, and it was in the simple form of a hand written note, it read: OPEN FROM 14TH AUGUST ONWARDS. Today was the 13th, which meant no pies for us. We looked around for signs of life in the desperate hope that maybe the proprietors were out the back baking a pre-opening batch of pies that they would let us have. No such luck. I couldn't get it out of my head how good the pies were meant to be, indeed good enough to die for, and we were only one day early. Drooling about the pies like Homer Simpson I momentarily pondered the idea of camping in the parking lot and waiting for the shop to open. But there wasn't much else in Pie Town and we were now competing against the clock. Disheartened we cycled back to the dirt track junction and rejoined the route. A couple of hundred yards up the trail was a very primitive RV site and we pulled in for water and a food break. The sign at the entrance to the site read FULL HOOK-UP, but out here it looked as though that meant just water and electricity which wouldn't have pleased our tetchy cable-addicted friend that we met back in Steamboat Springs. Lunch was body temperature processed cheese slices on day-old bread which was a far cry from the pies, cheesecake and ice cream I had promised my legs for getting me here. There was some good news though; it was time for a map change. We ate dinner sitting on the dusty ground and had map number six (the final one) spread out on the ground like a blanket at a picnic. The corners were held down with rapidly diminishing piles of cheese slices and stale bread. Once again there was an overlap of the maps and we managed to gain about six miles from it.

In stark contrast to our limp vegetarian fare, the route we were following formed a livestock trail that headed south through Star Wars terrain and connected Pie Town to the Beefsteak Trail (or the Magdalena Livestock Drive, to give it its proper name). The Beefsteak Trail was, in true Spaghetti Western style, the quintessential route along which cowboys herded their livestock. It linked the grazing lands of western New Mexico and eastern Arizona to the Magdalena railroad. In its heyday back in 1919 over 170,000 cattle and sheep were driven along it, and believe it or not it was still operational as late as the 1950s, thus making it the last cattle trail in regular use in the United States. Apparently the reason the ritual was continued for so long, even though both road and rail modes were in full operation, was that the beasts would get a lot of exercise and coupled with their continuous grazing they were in far better condition than those transported by rail and therefore got a higher price. In theory this sounds logical, but when I looked at myself, and I had had a lot of exercise and an awful lot of grazing, I didn't see a well-conditioned human specimen, rather I saw a skinny runt who would have been the last one to be sold at an auction.

The Great Divide route south of Pie Town stayed within close proximity of the Continental Divide and shortly after rejoining the dirt road we crossed the Continental Divide twice. Although they weren't climbs of any real magnitude, the pie debacle had taken the wind out of my sails, and as such the going was hard. Needless to say it was also a sore point with JK, who had been dreaming about his cherry pie for hours and found the cheese slice sandwiches a very poor substitute. Shortly after getting Continental Divide crossing number twenty out of the way we decided to set up camp bringing our day's total distance to eighty nine miles (I am sure that if we had had our pies we could have easily completed our goal of one hundred miles, and yes, I must let

150

go of the pie fiasco and move on). Supper was more stale bread and processed cheese washed down with black decaffeinated coffee. The mealtime conversation that evening centred on the injustice of not getting our well-earned pies.

***

Eddy's grating shrieks abruptly pulled me out my dream world (a world where the phrases ' Oh, I couldn't eat another pie...' and 'go on then, if you insist,' featured heavily), and with a start I awoke to find myself in the all too familiar blue dome. I blinked hard to clear my eyes of the gum that was sticking them closed. When they focussed I really wished I hadn't; JK was rolling around on his back, like an upturned turtle, trying desperately to put his shorts on. Apart from having only one calf in his shorts he was totally naked and as we had been sleeping top-to-tail, the view he presented was far from pleasing to the eye. Fortunately I was lying next to the tent exit and with a single move I unzipped the door and clambered outside. The view of the surrounding Mangas Mountains and the fresh air that was tinged with wild mint was far more agreeable.

Breakfast was the remnants of the process cheese slices and rock-hard crusts of bread that had been the theme of our last few meals. Although they tasted rank it was the last of our savoury food, unless of course you include the abhorrent bag of curry flavoured trail mix, that JK seemed reluctant to throw away.

Although I am sure the idea of eating chocolate and sugary pastries all day sounds good to most people, let me assure you that after a couple of hours it isn't. By the end of Breakfast C on most days, my teeth ached with a dull kind of pain as the enamel was being eaten away by a morning's worth of refined sugar. Usually at this point the very thought of eating more sweet, sugary junk food made me feel ill. But it had to be done, it was either that or bonk. This was usually the time when I started craving savoury food like fish, vegetables, or high fat foods like cheese. The reason for our poor quality diet was not through choice but because it was our only realistic option; chocolate bars and snacks are cheap, come ready packaged and are therefore easy to transport, and they contain a lot of energy. They were also the only ready available food that we routinely came across; gas station employees care as much about recommended daily intakes of vital nutrients as they do about personal hygiene. And so with my arm twisted up my back I sent a couple of Snickers down my oesophagus to join the cheesy chyme in my stomach, I then belched, and began our daily, southern pilgrimage.

The morning ride was very pleasant taking us along forest tracks and to make things even more enjoyable they generally headed in a downhill direction. But it wasn't long before the washboard track surface had returned and after several miles it was as if they had never been away. It was only when we crossed the paved State Highway 12 and the corrugations juxtaposed with the smoothness of the blacktop, that I realised how bad they actually were. My sojourn into a comfortable cycling world was very short lived, we literally just crossed the road and I was buffeted back onto a bone jarring surface that lasted the rest of the morning. My fondness of crossing the tarmac was completely different to that of the semi-feral cattle the cowboys drove along the Beefsteak Trail. The beasts would often refuse to cross the black top and would abruptly stop at the road's edge and paw at it. In order to coax the cattle across the cowboys would often resort to shovelling a strip of dirt over the road over which the bovines were happy to tread. It was amazing to think that this practice would have occurred very close to where we were as Old Horse Springs, an important water stop on the Beefsteak Trail, was situated only six miles due east on State Highway 12. After the crossing the route headed in a plumb line down the map and each pedal turn was taking us directly south. As we continued along the rutted track we skirted the edges of Plains of San Agustin which is a flat stretch of land 50 miles in diameter delineating a lakebed that harks back to the Pleistocene epoch. At some time or other the area was hit by a major meteorite storm and has since been a rich source of space rocks, giving the Star Wars ambience of this region a bit of credence. Adding further weight to the outer space theme is the nearby Very Large Array; a series of nearly thirty satellite dishes arranged in a Y-shape. The term Very Large is a suitable description for the configuration, as each arm of the Y reaches thirteen miles across the plain, and each dish has a diameter of eighty feet. Together they form the world's largest radio telescope and scan the universe for radio waves that were given off by stars and galaxies a staggering number of years ago. This was all going on out of sight to our left, and just as hard to believe in this flat wilderness, the Continental Divide was also snaking its way south about five miles to our right.

As we left the Plains of San Agustin behind we picked up a gorge whose proper name is La Jolla Canyon. It was good to be in the canyon as it meant it was pretty difficult to wander off course. Normally having said something like that we would subsequently get hopelessly lost, but for some reason we didn't and the canyon lead us, pinball style, into the Gila National Forest, across the Continental Divide twice, and up to a place called Collins Park. In stark contrast to the plains Collins Park was a beautiful forest of aspens and pine. However, as was becoming obvious, the landscapes of New Mexico don't stay the same for long and we were soon riding along grassy slopes in O-Bar-O Creek giving me a sense of déjà vu and reminding me of Helena, Montana. Fortunately we weren't as green as we were back then and due to a month's worth of acclimatisation and experience the riding was extremely pleasant and inspiring. The terrain morphed once more and we found ourselves riding through an arid, dusty rock strewn canyon, and then once again it changed and we were riding through juniper, oak and pine forests. The varied landscape served as an excellent distraction to the general toil we were putting in navigating the circuitous corrugated tracks that constitute this beautiful part of the Gila National Forest. Nonetheless the fatigue had been steadily accumulating and feeling somewhat weary at the eighty mile mark we checked the map for a suitable place to set up camp. We decided to push on for a further eight miles and settle down for the night at Wall Lake primitive campsite. As the name suggests it is situated next to Wall Lake, which in addition to being an excellent morning vista it would allow us to replenish our water stores. Regarding the track to Wall Lake, the map legend read: "Road is high grade but possibly washboarded," it should have read: "Road is medium grade and definitely washboarded." As we coasted down the slight decline to Wall Lake it looked perfect; a beautiful forest on the edge of spectacular lake. But the reality was a little different. Where the campsite symbol was on our map there had once been a campsite on the ground before us. We could tell this from circles of stones surrounding piles of ash which had at some stage been campfires. Only now the whole area either side of the track was bounded by a wire fence, off which hung unambiguous signs that read "PRIVATE LAND NO CAMPING." The light was beginning to fade and we hadn't seen anyone for hours, it was not like this track was a major thoroughfare so we decided we would have our evening meal and set up camp at last light. After all, we were going to be setting off first thing in the morning so no one would be any wiser.

We sat under a mature tree about twenty yards from the water's edge and cobbled together our usual hotchpotch of food that falls under the all-encompassing umbrella "supper". It was JK's turn to cook and he managed to locate an "emergency" dehydrated boil-in-the-bag pasta that had gone unnoticed in his rucksack. Had we known about its existence it wouldn't have survived this long. For culinary depth our energy-slurry was accompanied by half a packet of beyond stale Ritz crackers that he found buried in a mesh pocket on the side of his rucksack. God alone knows how long they had been there.

'Penne pasta in a luxurious cream of chicken sauce,' JK announced, placing the bag of partially cooked pasta on a nearby rock that acted as a table (we never fully cooked our pasta as it wasted far too much fuel). He had imaginatively crushed up the stale Ritz crackers and presented them with the rather grandiose title of 'finger nibbles.'

Finger nibbles they weren't. Stale Ritz crackers they were; the thin veneer was useless.

'They're awful,' he commented, and with that he poured them into the bag of pasta and gave the concoction a stir. I must admit the resultant paste tasted rather nice, in a kind of blue-cheese sort of way.

As the light was fading we pitched the tent and from our sleeping bags we watched the sun set behind the trees. Then to our dismay the silence was interrupted by the distant sound of a vehicle. It wasn't long before I could make out the pickup making its way up the track and I knew that in a few minutes it would be level with us, and it wasn't quite dark yet. The tyres crunched to halt on the track about twenty yards away.

'Excuse me. You can't camp there,' came a man's voice.

In some kind of childlike attempt at invisibility we lay silent and motionless. Reasoning had obviously left our rational minds because it didn't matter how still we were there was still an obvious blue tent.

'Excuse me. You can't camp there,' came the voice again.

We kept up the pretence a little longer and then on the third request we gave in.

JK clambered out of the tent and wandered over to the guy who, to me, was just a silhouette against the fiery sunset.

'It says on the map that it's a campsite,' JK feebly offered. Even from my vantage point (wrapped up in my sleeping bag with my head poking out of the tent entrance) and in the poor light I could read the NO CAMPING sign that was only a couple of yards away from our tent.

'It WAS,' came the stern reply, 'but that was over five years ago. A family friend bought the land and he has had a lot of trouble with campers, so it's no longer a campsite.'

He didn't offer us any alternative and the pregnant pause that had developed had become a little embarrassing.

JK broke the silence, 'What kind of trouble?'

'Folk getting drunk and letting off five hundred rounds, that sort of thing.'

JK diplomatically explained that we didn't have any beer let alone a firearm and that we would be breaking camp at first light. He seemed convinced that we would leave no trace of our stay, but said he would inform his friend about what we were doing. Fair enough. JK returned to the tent and he to his pick up.

As JK clambered back into his sleeping bag, the guy shouted, 'you really ought to get yourselves a gun, there's been a 350 pound bear roaming round these parts. Killed some livestock and we ain't caught him yet.'

Our flimsy tent sat in the middle of a wilderness that is home to a whole host of critters, from bats to, coyotes, foxes, skunks, raccoons, coatimundis, ringtail cats, weasels, bobcats, mountain lions, squirrels, rats, mice, and voles, along with a multitude of songbirds, plus turtles, frogs, lizards, and snakes. And of course this 350 pound bear. Whether he was pulling our legs or not we were unsure, but it didn't matter. With that irksome bit of knowledge running around my head I couldn't sleep despite my best efforts. Somewhere nearby something grunted, and we both squealed.

CHAPTER FOURTEEN. WALL LAKE TO ANTELOPE WELLS

'the spoils would be worth it'

There was no sign of the bear during the night and I can say that with authority, because I spent most of the night listening out for it. I can also confirm that JK had a sound night's sleep, and no doubt the knowledge that I was on watch duty contributed to his comfortable slumber. For some reason I couldn't convince myself to sleep even though I told myself, mantra style, how much I needed it. However, when Eddy signalled it was time to get up my body developed an overwhelming desire to roll over and crash out.

We started the ride pretty much on empty, just a cup of decaf and a Baby Ruth each. We were running very low on supplies, so I didn't even have a caffeine crutch to kick my sleep-deprived body into action. Fortunately my morale was bolstered as the morning trail took us along an inspirational natural corridor that bisected two wilderness expanses; on our right was the Gila Wilderness and on our left was the Aldo Leopold Wilderness. The Gila Wilderness was established in 1924 as the first forest wilderness preserve in the United States. It is a massive area of over 400,000 acres which is set amidst the even bigger Gila National Forest, which itself is over 2.7 million acres. To further cement my belief that New Mexico's landscape is as diverse as the endless permutations of chocolate bar you can find in any American gas station, located within the wilderness were deep canyons, cliffs, hot springs, streams and vegetation ranging from desert agave to thick forests of spruce and fir. Wilderness was the perfect description and the only indications that we were in the present were the cutting-edge bikes that we were riding and the equipment we were carrying, but for them, I had the impression that little had changed for centuries. During one of our food breaks I had a moment to admire the natural grandeur of the wilderness and be taken aback by its vastness. As I scanned the area I wondered whether what I could see now would have been the same vista the Mogollon Indians, who resided in this area nearly 700 years ago, would have seen. If so, it was only the displacement of seven centuries that separated us, everything else was the same. To the east of the corridor sits the Black Range which rises from the desert sands and stands as a prominent land feature. A nature enthusiast called Aldo Leopold keenly forested this portion of the original Gila Wilderness and in recognition of his efforts this section of the wilderness was named in his honour. Other, more famous individuals have also frequented these parts; the vastness, diversity and maze-like topography of the area meant that it was an ideal refuge for fugitives, and the list of outlaws reads like who's who of renegade Apache Indian chiefs including: Geronimo, Cochise and Mangas Coloradas.

A few miles further south we climbed up on to the Continental Divide for the twenty fifth time since our journey began over five weeks ago. It was only a short ascent and then our route followed the Continental Divide for about eight miles. As well as delineating the flow of water to the west or east, this section of the Continental Divide also marked the boundaries of the two wilderness areas. Needless to say the views were awesome and coupled with the effortless level riding, I found myself in mountain biking Nirvana. Being on top of the Continental Divide meant all destinations were downhill and after an hour's worth of excellent ridge riding we peeled off south on State Highway 35. The Continental Divide simultaneously snaked off in a southwesterly direction. State Highway 35 took us downhill for an eight mile coast along the picturesque Mimbres river valley to the small town of Mimbres. It was in this valley that the Mimbres Indians, a branch of the Mogollon tribe, lived alongside the Anasazi Indians from 850 AD to the turn of the thirteenth century. The legacy of the Mimbres Indians can still be found in the area in the form of abandoned villages, farming lands, and hot springs. But unfortunately most of the ruins have been destroyed by pothunters.

According to our map Mimbres had it all, a trolley symbol and a knife and fork. The Great Divide route swings west just before Mimbres but with the lure of food it was easy to justify putting in a few extra pedal strokes to get my hands on some real food. After a couple of hundred yards a mercantile came into view and it was open. We cycled past hoping to see what warranted the knife and fork symbol; maybe it was a café, or a restaurant. We gave it a couple more hundred yards but our limited search was fruitless and with the tangible bounty at the mercantile preying on our minds we swung the bikes around and headed back to the shop. Lunch A was barbeque flavoured crisp butties washed down with Gatorade. It wasn't the real food I was after, but it tasted damn good. Lunch B was Ritz crackers and guacamole dip. Whilst we were having Lunch C, a full tub of Ben and Jerry's each, a couple of guys pulled up on mountain bikes. They were towing trailers and had the well-beaten Great Divide look about them, but they had come from the wrong direction. Perhaps they had made a map error. I smugly spooned some ice cream into my mouth and mentally patted myself on the back for our near flawless navigation of the route.

'Hi, I'm Mark, this is Pat,' said the first guy offering his grubby gloved hand,

'John,' I replied shaking it with an even grubbier hand, 'and this is JK,' I added nodding in his direction.

157

Mark and Pat were suitably impressed with how light we were travelling and I smugly spooned some more ice cream into my mouth as JK recounted our story and how quick we were covering the ground. They were following the recommended distances in the trail notes and I kept giving confirmatory looks as JK told them about the century rides we had put in. I nodded in agreement in all the right places whilst spooning in the ice cream; slow, smooth and cool. Then came the first sucker punch.

In a far too casual tone, Mark commented, 'I take it you didn't fancy the café then?'

'What?' JK blurted.

'Yeah, it's just around the corner,' Pat interjected, pointing down the road from where he had come. Then he sucker punched us again with an offhand, 'they do some real good pie there.'

I choked on my ice cream and had to spit it out on the veranda. 'Pie,' I said sternly, wiping the ice cream that was now dripping from my nostrils, 'I've been after pie ever since the shop in Pie Town was closed.'

Then came the knockout punch.

'Oh, you didn't stop at the first shop in Pie Town did you?' Mark asked, then added 'The Pie-O-Neer Café is a little further on, and it was open.'

I felt dizzy and slumped back in my chair. If only we had gone a little further, both today and in Pie Town. And then the realisation hit me, maybe all of the other places we couldn't find on the maps and had cursed the cartographers about actually existed, we probably just hadn't looked hard enough. Mark and Pat set off for Silver City, and as I shook hands with Mark he looked wistfully into the air and commented to no one in particular, 'and they do a good blueberry cheesecake at the Pie-O-Neer.'

I momentarily thought about heading up the road to café and having some cheesecake, but when I stood up my distended belly groaned in laden protest and I was forced to change my mind. I had to accept the fact that it was going to be another cheesecake and pieless day, and I would have to learn to live with the fact that it was all our own fault. The extra distances we would have had to ride, both at Pie Town and today amounted to no more than five miles, or less than three tenths of one percent of our overall journey. The benefit to morale for that extra effort would have been immeasurable. With the second-rate crisp-buttie lunch sitting heavy I cocked my leg over Corsair and attempted the final noteworthy climb of the entire route; a 1000 foot ridge climb out of Mimbres. We then coasted down to State Highway 152 and followed it on an easterly bearing for three miles to the small town of Hanover. According to the map the ride to the next town, Silver City, should have been easy – a nice runoff from Hanover followed by a six mile flat tarmac ride. The reality was slightly different, but the phase shift wasn't as big as it had been in the past. The level ride was actually a series of rollers and the giant was back to his usual antagonistic tricks. But knowing Silver City wasn't far off we dropped the pace and enjoyed the ride in. Things were agreeable up to when our strip of tarmac became the multi-lane Federal Highway 180. Very quickly the pecking order of the road was explained to me by a juggernaut; cyclists were at the bottom of the hierarchy. We wrestled with the traffic for several adrenaline-fuelled miles until we reached the tranquil oasis of Silver City RV campsite.

A staggeringly beautiful receptionist checked us into the RV Park and gave us directions for pitching our tent.

'You can put it up over there on that piece of lawn near the sprinklers,' she said pointing out of a side window. Already on the lawn were a tent and a couple of bikes that looked like Mark and Pat's.

'Don't worry I won't turn the sprinklers on,' she added laughing.

Mesmerised by her beauty, JK engaged in a bit of banter, 'you can if you like, I could do with a hose down,' he said with more than a tinge of machismo.

'Well if you like, I can hose you down proper out the back,' she countered coolly calling his bluff.

'Er, er,' JK stammered, and then added incredulously, 'I don't think the cold water will do my old joints any good.' He then made a hasty retreat. Or he would have done if he hadn't made several attempts to push open the sliding door.

We wandered over to our designated camping area and pitched our tent next to Mark and Pat's. There was no sign of them so we headed into Silver City in search of a tyre and some food. By chance we stumbled across Gila Hike and Bike and at long last I was able to get my hands on a new rear tyre. There wasn't much of the Great Divide journey left, but knowing my luck if I didn't buy a replacement now the bald tyre would split within a hundred miles or so and we would be scuppered. With my puncture paranoia quashed we made our way to Adobe Springs Café and sampled their Mexican cuisine. It was getting dark by the time we got back to the campsite and Mark and Pat were sitting at a picnic table near the tents poring over the final leg of their journey. With the hardest stuff behind us and being in the company of the last two Great Divide cyclists we were likely to encounter on the route, we opted to join them. The beer and the banter flowed. I momentarily thought about the professional cyclist ethos but it vaporised as soon as I popped off the bottle top of my Budweiser. It was only when I was getting a beer-buzz that I remembered I had to fit the new tyre to Corsair. I can't remember too much of the details so I assume the mechanics went on okay.

For a while now we had been getting increasingly concerned about how we were going to get to El Paso from the border without having to cycle it. We had an internal flight to catch from El Paso to Atlanta before retracing our steps back to England. Mark and Pat who were both Americans were lucky enough to have a relative who was willing to pick them and their bikes up and drive them back home. They suggested we ring Adventure Cycling from the border and see what options other folk have used.

Perhaps fearing that we were trying to blag a free lift, Mark swiftly changed the conversation and asked us whether we had come across a Polish rider on our travels.

'He had a pet rat in his trailer, you couldn't miss him,' he said.

'The last time we saw him he was heading into A & M Reservoir with only one water bladder and a bottle,' added Pat.

By all accounts we should have overtaken him and it would have been nice to meet the eccentric guy and his rodent friend, but in their absence we toasted them and hoped they were all right. Perhaps they met up with Vince and are all living happily ever after. Our companions were taking a day off in Silver City before the final push and weren't overly concerned about having a hangover. The beer was already getting the better of us, so with phenomenal restraint we left Mark and Pat to continue drinking into the night and headed to the fetid blue dome for a well-earned sleep.

***

We mutedly broke camp in the early morning stillness. For me the silence was for two reasons, first I didn't want to wake Mark and Pat, but on a more visceral level I was aware that this was to be our penultimate day on the trail and I wasn't sure how I felt about it. Part of me wanted to complete the task I had started, but an equal part wanted to keep going. I was enjoying the adventure, riding new trails each day, literally not knowing what was round the corner. Our tyres crunched along the driveway of the RV Park and we exited under a sign that read, 'Vaya con dios,' which was just as well because when we turned onto State Highway 90 the early morning Silver City traffic was as bad as ever.

Silver City was originally an Old West outpost that proliferated in the 1870s as a result of the now familiar silver strike that has kick-started life in most of these Wild West towns. With the prosperity came the drinking, the gambling, the whoring and the robbing. One of Silver City's claims to fame is that it spawned one of the Wild West's most famous sons, Billy the Kid. Billy lived in Silver City and began his criminal career in his mid-teens when he held up a Chinese laundry. His resulting incarceration also heralded his inaugural jailbreak when he seized the moment and climbed out of the jailhouse chimney. Six years later Billy the Kid was shot dead by Sheriff Pat Garrett, but in those short intervening years he managed to get himself the reputation of being one of America's most vicious and ruthless killers. Apart from the Billy the Kid touristy reminders, Silver City appeared very modern and to me in no way reflected its Wild West past. However Pinos Altos, situated less than ten miles north of the city, looks like it has come right out of a silver screen western, with its adobe buildings and Wild West ambiance. Pinos Altos, like Silver City, also has a chequered past, and in the early 1860s it was the site of a raid by hundreds of Apache Indians on the townsfolk. Three miners and fifteen Indians were killed in the conflict.

South of Silver City the Continental Divide stayed within about four miles of State Highway 90, both of which generally headed in a southerly direction. Despite the close proximity of the Continental Divide we were slowly losing height and were now generally cruising at an altitude of 6,000 feet – approximately half the height of Indiana Pass back in Colorado. I gave a smile in recognition of my isosceles triangle theory, it had taken thirty six days to come to fruition but I was finally getting a bit of payback. The trail notes contained words of encouragement suggesting that as we left Silver City we would also leave the mountains behind, but it also gave words of caution predicting that the temperatures we were about to experience were to be hotter than any we had previously encountered. True to form the temperature was climbing, but it was still morning and so was manageable. What's more with a tailwind, gentle decline and the smooth paved highway we weren't having to exert ourselves and weren't suffering in the heat. After twenty pleasurable miles we turned off the blacktop and onto a washboard dirt track that headed into the Chihuahuan Desert. A gentle climb then took us through tall yucca forests and joined the Continental Divide allowing us to ride along its spine for several miles.

The wind picked up as we dropped down from the Continental Divide and in the distance towards where we were heading it had whipped itself into a sandstorm. We decided to stop for a quick map reference to check we were on the right path as it was looking like navigation was doing to be difficult in the dust bowl. We also took the opportunity to fashion our bandanas over our noses and mouths bandit-style to protect ourselves from the dirt and sand. Lamentably our map reference confirmed that we had to pass through the storm to get to Separ, and with our heads down we pedalled in the swirling sand and made slow progress for almost an hour. I receded into my familiar mantra-world of watching my knees rise and fall. Almost as quick as it had whipped itself into a frenzy the sandstorm disappeared. In the distance I could just make out juggernaut shapes inching their way across the horizon like lumbering dinosaurs. A freight train of staggering length was crawling towards our trail, meaning that we had to get to the other side of the railway line before it crossed our path otherwise we would literally have to wait hours for it to pass. To beat the train was going to necessitate a fair old amount of effort, but the spoils would be worth it, because on the other side of the tracks was Separ, a small town with a knife and fork symbol next to it on the map. In true Indiana Jones style we just made it across the tracks in front of the engine and in doing so we instantaneously eased off the pedalling and cruised to the gas station-cum-mercantile that was situated on main highway.

We sat on the shop veranda and munched our way through pre-packaged sandwiches, ice cream, and bottles of Gatorade of varying colours.

'Do y'know it's only seventy miles to Antelope Wells from here,' JK commented whilst pouring over the final map.

'I'm not sure I like your line of thought,' I joked.

'So, what do you reckon?' he pursued.

'What? Clip the lot today?'

He nodded whilst chewing on an entire sandwich.

'It's doable. We could put in a big one today, camp at the border and take it from there,' I thought out loud. Then after doing a bit of mental arithmetic added, 'and if we get there before ten, we will have done it inside double Stamstad's time.'

'Easy, it's all flat and on road from here,' JK added tracing the route on the map with his finger.

With that we wolfed down the remaining food, restocked our supplies and got back on the bikes.

We picked up State Highway 146, which made a plumb line for the border and in doing so passed a road sign confirming that we were on the correct road for Antelope Wells. The signpost was the first tangible thing I'd seen regarding our fabled destination. Of course I'd seen it on the map, but I had just passed a sign with the words emblazoned on it a couple of feet tall. I was buoyed that the place actually existed, and bizarrely it reminded me of Bognor Regis. As a youngster I had heard the place name Bognor Regis and, because to me it was a silly name, I had assumed it was a fictitious place (I also used to think the same about Coventry) but then whilst I was living in West Sussex you can imagine my surprise when one day I accidentally drove into the town.

162

Seeing the Antelope Wells sign and knowing that we were going to be there that night put some verve into our legs and we rode down the highway never dropping below twenty miles per hour. Somewhere along this stretch we crossed the Continental Divide for our twenty seventh and final time. It wasn't long before we arrived at Hachita ("little hatchet"), the last settlement on route to the border, and had a pit stop to refuel before our final push. The café at Hachita is just what a weary trailhound needs, decent home-cooked food in a laidback and friendly atmosphere. I opted for the seafood stir-fry and whilst it was being cooked I headed outside to a phone booth I had seen on the way in to contact Adventure Cycling about possible travel arrangements from the border.

'Adventure Cycling, how can I help?'

'Hi, I'm doing the Great Divide Route and I am just wondering what transport options there are for getting to El Paso from Antelope Wells.'

'I can give you some numbers you can ring to arrange a pick up, but you're better off phoning when you're a couple of weeks off the border so that you can negotiate a time to meet. It's not economical just to pick up the odd rider.'

Ah, he was assuming I was a sensible person. It just dawned on me how stupid the situation was; I had just ridden two and a half thousand miles across America and left it to the last minute to work out how I was going to get back.

'The thing is,' I began, 'I am a couple of hours from the border and...'

'Well, give it a few weeks and try those numbers...'

'No, not that border. Not Port Roosville, I'm just outside of Antelope Wells. I'm just about to finish.' I felt like the idiot that I was. Give him his due he didn't laugh.

'Well the only option you've got is to wait at the border for other riders I suppose, and then share a lift, or...'

'Or?'

'Or cycle the 140 odd miles to El Paso.'

I was feeling distinctly uneasy by the situation and I tried to salvage a bit of self-respect by saying, 'cool, yeah we'll ride it.'

I don't think he was fooled.

I entered the café a little despondent at the thought of having to backtrack a hundred and odd miles. But JK couldn't have felt more different.

'I've sorted it,' he enthused between bites of burrito, 'Alma has phoned Sam and he'll be here in a minute.'

'Who's Alma? Who's Sam?' I asked incredulously.

163

JK beckoned for me to sit down and pointing to his mouth and using other gesticulations informed me that his burrito was his number one priority and that everything was in hand. Not convinced I tucked into my seafood stir-fry.

'Alma runs the café and she's just phoned a guy called Sam who drives a pickup and will probably give us a lift. He'll be here in a few minutes,' JK finally informed me.

After a few rounds of coffee and pie, a pickup screeched to a halt in a cloud of dust outside the café and a weather-beaten old cowboy got out and headed in our direction. The door opened and the stranger filled it.

'Hi Sam,' Alma enthused, 'these are the guys I was talking about.'

Sam walked over to our table.

'John Metcalfe,' I said extending my arm.

'Can't shake,' he said showing me his palms, 'I've got some sort of skin disease.'

I nodded trying my best to contain my shock at the peeling skin. He dropped a business card on our table and pulled up a chair. The card read:

Tires – Land – Whiskey – Manure – Guns – Gold – Snake Oil – Used Cars – Birth Control Pills – Mining claims – Mules – Revolutions Started – Assassinations Plotted – Uprisings Quelled – Dictators Replaced – Tigers Tamed – Bars Emptied – Virgin Conversion – Tax Free Investments.

-SAM HARRY-

Prospector, Treasure Hunter

It looked like Uncle Sam was our man. We plied the 76 year old gentleman with coffee and made affable chitchat with him, but we were skirting around the hard fact that we wanted to know: how much was it going to cost? Although we were entirely dependant on Uncle Sam and had to pay whatever he asked there wasn't that over the barrel feeling that I had experienced in Helena. Eventually our conversation meandered its way towards fixing a price and Uncle Sam was the first to put a figure to it.

'I'll pick you and your bikes up tomorrow from the border for…' he paused fingering his coffee cup, '…let's say 150 bucks.'

We faked a bit of deliberation, but quickly took him up on his offer.

'I will see you gentlemen at the border tomorrow at noon,' and with that he got up and made his way to his pickup.

'That's even cheaper than the lift from Whitefish to the start,' JK commented draining his coffee.

I was looking out of the window at a beat up car in the parking lot outside of the café. It had a bumper sticker, similar to the one I had seen in Seattle, that read, DESTINATIONS ARE OVERRATED.

'See that?' I said to JK nodding in the direction of the car.

'See what?'

'The sticker.'

'Yeah,' he said contemplatively.

'How about we doss down here tonight and instead of busting our balls riding to the border tonight we enjoy the cruise in tomorrow morning?' I inquired.

'What about doing it inside double Stamstad's time?' JK quizzed in a surprised tone.

'I dunno, it doesn't seem to matter that much for some reason.'

'I'm cool with that. It was your daft idea anyhow,' he said, and responded by beckoning to Alma that a round of coffees was in order.

We pitched the tent outside of the café and were treated to a distant lightning storm before we retired to the tent for the last time.

***

We broke camp and had everything packed up on Vick and Corsair in record time. It was kind of ironic that now that our camping procedures had become autonomous it was also to be our last day of performing them. Within half an hour of waking we were heading down State Highway 81, a lonely road that cuts through the arid Chihuahuan Desert and crosses into Mexico at the Antelope Wells border checkpoint. In true Great Divide style we were heading into a bitch of a headwind, but it was somehow befitting of our entire journey and I wouldn't have had it any other way. Who was I kidding? Barely an hour into the morning ride I was berating myself for not continuing to the border the previous night when the weather was calm and cool. The road stretched on in front of us all of the way to the shimmering horizon and would have been a monotonous head torture had it not been for the roadside mile markers indicating our distance from the border: 40…39…38 miles to go. These were paltry figures compared to the remaining miles we had on our first camp at Tuchuck campground, Montana. How my mental state had changed from that first night when I thought the whole distance was simply too much. Mile by mile we had steadily eaten into the staggering total of 2470 miles and now we were down to just double figures.

Deserts are generally classified by having less than twelve inches of annual precipitation and although the Chihuahuan Desert conforms to this it is still able to support a wide variety of flora and fauna. We rode past numerous species of plants including creosote bush, lechuguilla, yucca and of course the ubiquitous cacti of which there are over sixty varieties in the Chihuahuan Desert. Most of the fauna in the desert are, understandably, nocturnal and avoid the midday sun, nonetheless I nearly managed to run over an example of one particular species. I was riding along and contemplating a funny looking spiral stick on the road ahead and it was only when I was a few feet away from it that I realised it was a rattlesnake.

'Shit!' I shouted and swerved out of the way at the last moment.

'They're all over place!' JK said, 'look.'

There was a knot of rattlers coiled up at the edge of the road, but fortunately being cold-blooded reptiles they were pretty docile after a cold night in the desert. They must have been lying on the warm blacktop in order to raise their body temperatures. To get bitten out here could be fatal as we had not seen another soul all morning. Nervously we continued along the crown of the road.

With about ten miles to go Uncle Sam overtook us on his way to the border leaving the Doppler effect of his horn in his wake. And shortly afterwards the squat buildings of the border checkpoint appeared on the horizon. JK pulled up alongside me.

'Well this is it mate,' he said, offering his hand for a high five, 'thanks for the ride.'

'You too,' I replied and slapped his hand, 'I can't believe that's it.'

Half an hour later, at 11:00 am we pulled into the border checkpoint.

The air-conditioned checkpoint was an excellent antidote to the searing heat outside.

'You've just finished the Great Divide right?' the customs official asked.

'Sure have,' JK replied.

'You're the first we've had in this year. You better get yourself a Coke,' he said, nodding towards a vending machine as if reading our minds.

I traded a couple of dollars with the machine for two ice cold Cokes.

'We've got some spare doughnuts here if your want some,' the official offered. We didn't need asking twice.

I don't know why, but I was somehow expecting more than just Coke and doughnuts when I had finished. Perhaps a medal; a round of "For he's a jolly good fellow" before being lofted into the air by a large and appreciative crowd with the accompanying chants of "Hip, hip hooray"; failing that a small welcoming party perhaps an interview for the local paper would have done. But no, there was nothing.

Uncle Sam was conspicuous by his absence, he had overtaken us and there hadn't been any side roads for him to take. Nonetheless I felt confident he would honour his word. The officials at the checkpoint were helpful and enthusiastic about our journey. They stamped our maps and took the obligatory photographs of us at the border. As I straddled the border of the two countries the wealth of each was starkly represented by the quality of the checkpoints. The American building was modern and clean, the Mexican one was rundown and from the outside looked as though it had been abandoned. That said, on the face of it both checkpoints seemed a little futile. They only controlled the road, either side of the blacktop was miles upon miles of desert. Then again I suppose if you're trying to cross the border illegally or smuggle black-market goods, and you use the road then you deserve to get caught. Ten minutes later, true to his word, Uncle Sam turned up and we put our gear in the back of his pickup and made our way back up State Highway 81 heading for El Paso airport.

'the key is knowing that it exists'

We sped back along State Highway 81 and covered the same distance as our morning ride in less than a fifth of the time. It was the first time we had been in a car since Dick Dodge gave us a lift to Anaconda, but within minutes the creature comforts of modern day living felt like they had never been away; a radio, air conditioning, electric this and electric that. As we raced along I noticed that the knot of rattlers had disappeared from the roadside, presumably because they had now got their body temperature up to operational speed. Or perhaps it was to avoid the rubbish that Uncle Sam casually disposed of through his open window with an autonomy that reflected years of thoughtless repetition.

'Little bastards they are,' he said referring to the snakes and lifting up the cassette tape housing lid situated between the two front seats. He revealed a revolver and added, 'I always carry this. Shoot them whenever I can.'

Apparently my near altercation with the rattler that morning would have, if the snake hadn't been docile, resulted in it striking out at the nearest thing possible, which would have probably been Corsair's tyre. This sounded pretty innocuous but Uncle Sam warned, 'a similar thing happened to a guy the other year, only one of the rattler's fangs broke off in his tyre and gave the guy a slow puncture. Hours later when he was mending it and was running his hand around the tyre checking for thorns...' he paused momentarily to light up a Marlboro, inhaled and continued, 'he pricked himself on the fang and got a dose of the venom.' He took another drag on the cigarette, slowly exhaled and added indifferently, 'don't know whether he lived or died.'

Sobering thought; I made a mental note to throw my tyres away if they were deflated by the time we got to El Paso. Hatchita came and went in the blink of an eye and before long we were on State Highway 9 heading straight for El Paso. Gradually the desert landscape became increasingly urban until we were driving through the billboards, high-rises and motels of downtown El Paso. El Paso is on the American-Mexico border and in stark contrast to the affluent American skyline within a stone's throw was the relative Mexican shantytown Ciudad Juarez. If I lived there I would be fairly pissed off, not necessarily because I had it so bad, but because others so obviously had it so good. And the fact that I would be reminded of it on a daily basis wouldn't help either. Uncle Sam dropped us off at the airport, helped us unpack and with a nod of the head and a 'good luck' he was gone. We wheeled the bikes into the airport and were ins transported, like aliens into a foreign land, back into the hustle and bustle of city life. Within ten minutes five people had bumped into me as they scurried along in their busy lives, and two people had pushed in front of us in the check-in queue.

As I stood in the queue the reward for my efforts became glaringly apparent. There was no need for a welcoming party, dancing girls or any recognition for my toil. There was no need for photographers, mayor's handshakes or exclusive magazine interviews. Moreover it wasn't about being a professional cyclist. No, it was all very simple. As I looked around the departure lounge at everyone's frenetic, pre-packaged, target-led lives the reward slotted into place. The return for my efforts was being able to step off the treadmill, albeit for a diminutive timeframe, but step off it I did nonetheless. I was afforded the opportunity to take a sabbatical from my normal existence and sample a parallel lifestyle, one that was simple, beautiful, and rewarding. As I stood in the queue aware that my time in the other world was over, I was envious that for others – the lone Australian cyclist, Rosie and Stuart, and others the world over – their visas for travel in this wonderful place were still valid. I also took solace in the thought that it is a welcoming parallel universe which I would certainly be revisiting at some stage in the future. The key is knowing that it exists.

We were at the head of the queue and were summoned to the check-in desk by a clerk. Having completed the Great Divide we were in El Paso ahead of schedule and we enquired whether we could bring our flights forward a couple of days, still allowing time to wander around El Paso and Mexico. The administrator was pleasant in a robotic sort of way but that wasn't an issue because our tickets were changed with a nominal administration charge. However the bikes were a different story. Apparently they were one inch too long and as such a $150 charge had to be levied for each of them. I argued that I was five kilograms lighter than when I flew out of England and that with the combined weight of Corsair and myself we didn't weigh as much as any of the other overweight passengers standing behind me in the queue.

I was greeted with, 'rules are rules, Sir.'

An inch; there was none of this illogical nonsense when trying to squeeze our bikes into Charlie's van, or Dick's or Uncle Sam's for that matter. However it prepared us nicely for our re-entry into the bureaucracy that is modern day living.

First things first. We had to get drunk on tequila and that's exactly what we did. I had also promised myself a pizza (in fact it was the one I had promised myself in the town of Cuba) and that's exactly what I ate. Unfortunately it was in that order and in very

...nsisted on getting a commemorative tattoo, and that's exactly what ...queasy couple of hours propped up in a dingy tattoo parlour belching a ...uila and pizza in a manner befitting some one who is slightly drunk, un... ...tching blood drip down JK's arm as the electronic needle was dragged across ...s skin. It may have looked like a ropey place to get something as permanent as a tattoo, but the artist who was plying his trade on JK's skin certainly looked the part; he had a full body suit of tattoos. This fits in nicely with my 'never eat anything that a thin chef prepares' philosophy; fat chefs by inference must eat their own food and enjoy it. A tattoo artist with bare skin somehow doesn't bode well; they've got to be able to walk the walk as well as talk the talk. This one even had a burrito hanging out of his mouth which bounced up and down like a cigarette as he talked. I wasn't sure whether it was the tequila, the loss of blood or the wafting burrito that was responsible for JK's nauseous expression. All three were responsible for mine.

***

Two days and one flight later we were sitting in Houlihan's bar in Atlanta airport awaiting our flight back to Manchester. We were sitting at the exact same table that we had dined at a little over five weeks ago. In fact I had ordered the same food as I had done. Our displacement was zero. Clean, refreshed and well fed the fatigue and toil of the previous weeks seemed like a distant memory, indeed almost as if someone had told me it had happened to them. It was impossible to conjure up the feelings of intense heat, fatigue and exhaustion that we had endured.

'I don't feel any different now than when we were last here,' I said to JK, 'I mean did we actually do the Divide or what?'

JK pulled up the sleeve of his T-shirt to reveal a tender looking strip of skin that was sporting an Aztec design. Wincing he confirmed, 'oh yes, we did it all right. You don't ride that far without forgetting it.'

But I almost had. I hadn't forgotten the route, the scenery or the people, nor had I forgotten the sensations or the feelings. But what had diminished were the intensities of those feelings. I had forgotten the horrors, the disappointments and the hard work. True to form my long-term memory was failing, and unfortunately it enjoys an inverse relationship with my professional cyclist dream. I drained my bottle of Budweiser, relaxed back in my chair. And having learned nothing I commented, 'Next time, we'll do it quicker...'

I hope you enjoyed reading this book. If you did, please write a review on your favou~~~ website.

Thanks

John

johnmetcalfewriting@gmail.com
Follow me on Twitter: @Johnny_Met
www.johnmetcalfewriting.wordpress.com

JOHN METCALFE

‹E FITNESS TRAINING

JOHN METCALFE

'Honest and straightforward to read
...plenty of useful fitness and training tips for all cyclists.'
- CYCLING WEEKLY

ISBN: 1840188588

Mountain Bike Fitness Training is a comprehensive manual for recreational or competitive mountain bikers wishing to enhance their performance in off-road riding. It is also a valuable resource for those who, wanting to improve their general fitness, have chosen the sport of mountain biking as a fun way to develop better health.

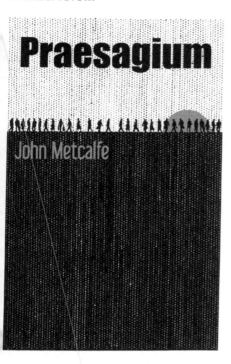

ASIN : B00E7Z6QEI

It's always easy to trace the breadcrumb trail backwards and note the causes retrospectively, but what if you could see the signs beforehand? What if you could filter out the noise? Could you tune into weak signals and know the future? Lee believed you could. What's more he was proving it could be done in some of the most unpredictable environments.

Praesagium follows three strangers who are preoccupied with their own futures. But when their paths cross in Mexico none of them had foreseen the outcome...

Made in the USA
Coppell, TX
01 August 2022